Go Grammar!

Teacher's Edition
Red Level

Marc Collins
Adrian Collins

Harcourt Achieve

Rigby • Saxon • Steck-Vaughn

www.HarcourtAchieve.com
1.800.531.5015

Go Grammar! Red Level Teacher's Edition
Steck-Vaughn Language Arts Solutions

© 2002 Thomson Learning Australia
Exclusive United States Distribution: Harcourt Achieve Inc.

© 2006 Harcourt Achieve Inc.

3 4 5 6 7 8 9 10 11 355 11 10 09 08 07 06

Printed in the United States of America

ISBN 1-4190-1243-6

Contents

Go Grammar! iii

Go Grammar!

A Simple, Flexible Solution for Grammar and Composition Support

Homework
Assign meaningful, student-centered homework that can be completed in a single sitting.

Practice
Assign independent practice for core grammar and composition concepts.

Enrichment
Provide students with opportunities for deeper study.

Remediation
Target certain concepts or skills that need further attention.

Reinforcement/ Review
Support and review key topics from your curriculum.

Core Grammar and Composition Instruction

Go Grammar! provides activity-based instruction for the skills that matter most, including . . .

- Understanding the parts of speech and their proper usage

- Using punctuation for correctness and clarity

- Identifying common errors in mechanics and usage

- Understanding phrases, clauses, and sentences

- Understanding the structure of different kinds of paragraphs

- Analyzing language and understanding its connection to audience

- Using roots, affixes, and mnemonics to improve spelling

Sequential Composition Instruction

In addition, the *Go Grammar!* series provides sequential support for the fundamentals of composition—starting with the basics of sentences and paragraphs in *Go Grammar!* Red Level and ending with complete essays in *Go Grammar!* Blue Level.

Clear, Student-Friendly Lessons

Each lesson in *Go Grammar!* begins with a **short explanation** followed by **three exercises**.

Students learn the basics of the lesson through simple explanations and clear examples.

Students then move on to complete three exercises that provide careful, student-friendly guidance in understanding the lesson.

3-Step Exercise Format

The carefully designed exercise format guides students step-by-step through each lesson, moving students from basic understanding to real-world application.

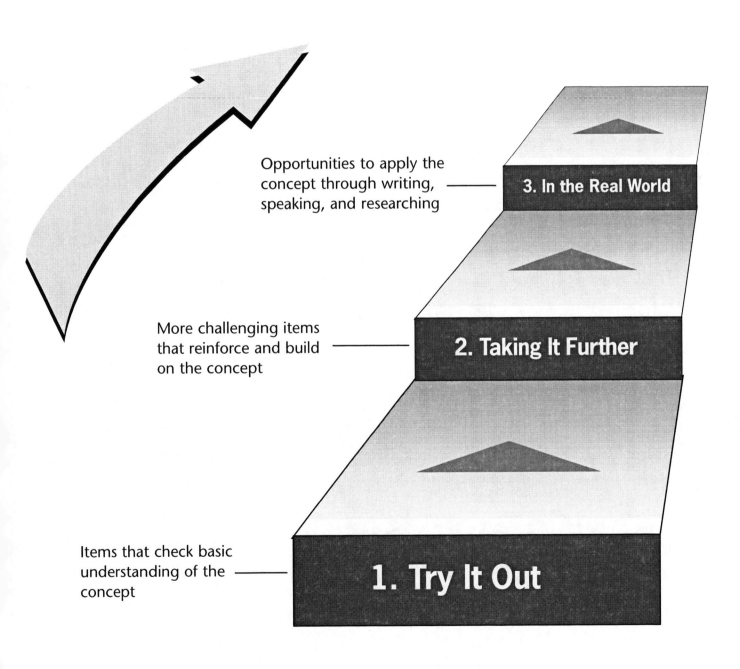

Opportunities to apply the concept through writing, speaking, and researching — **3. In the Real World**

More challenging items that reinforce and build on the concept — **2. Taking It Further**

Items that check basic understanding of the concept — **1. Try It Out**

LESSON 1 · Common Nouns

NOUNS

A **common noun** is a word that names a person, place, thing, feeling, idea, or quality.

Example The **students** have the **confidence** to complete their **assignment** on **dinosaurs**.

You capitalize a common noun when it starts a sentence.

Example **Students** gain confidence in writing by practicing frequently.

Try It Out

1 Use the letters in the grid below to spell at least six common nouns of three letters or more. You must use the middle letter P somewhere in each word. Each letter can be used only once in a word. No plurals ending in -s are allowed.

T	I	N
O	P	A
A	S	T

Answers may vary.

pain, paint, past, pasta, pat, patio, piano, pint, point, post, soap,

span, spot, stop, tap

2 Now write a sentence or two about something that happened when you were younger. Include at least four nouns from the word game and underline them.

Answers will vary.

_____

_____

_____

_____

Taking It Further

Here are two ways to identify a noun.

i If you can put *a*, *an*, or *the* before a word, that word is a noun.

> **Example**   I like riding **a** bike.

ii If a word can be made plural (more than one) by adding an *s*, then that word is a noun.

> **Example**   I like riding bike**s**.

Look for nouns in a book or newspaper. Write down at least two common nouns in each column below.

Sample answers.

Person	Place	Animal	Thing	Feeling	Idea
grandmother	hill	giraffe	bike	sadness	fairness
friend	home	bird	box	sympathy	freedom

In the Real World

Imagine that you want to sell something you own, like a musical instrument or some sporting goods. Compose a brief advertisement below to put in a local newspaper. Use fewer than 20 words, and include at least three common nouns.

> **Example**   Second-hand baseball <u>bat</u> for <u>sale</u>. First-grade <u>wood</u> with a good <u>grip</u>.

Answers will vary.

_____

_____

_____

_____

LESSON (2) Proper Nouns

NOUNS

Proper nouns name a particular person, place, or thing.

Example **Tiger Woods** is an elite athlete.
The **Federal Reserve** employs hundreds of people.

They also name the days and months (but not seasons).

Example I can't wait for winter to come in **December**.

Proper nouns always start with a capital letter, either in a sentence or standing alone.

Example **Skytrek Airlines** has flights to **Alaska**.

Try It Out

Answer the quiz using proper nouns. Remember to use capital letters where necessary.

| Sample answers. |

1 Name a famous landmark in Washington, D.C. _Lincoln Memorial_____

2 Name your favorite sports team. _Cleveland Browns_____

3 What is the capital city of your state? _Austin_____

4 Who won the last World Series? _Boston Red Sox_____

5 Name a mountain range. _the Himalayas, the Rocky Mountains_____

6 Name a country that has a desert in it. _China, Australia_____

7 Sea World is a place where you can go on rides and see lots of sea animals. Name another place where you can go for entertainment. _Disneyland, National Zoo_____

8 Name a river that is not in the United States. _the Nile_____

Taking It Further

The following e-mail exchange between friends does not capitalize proper nouns. Rewrite it with capital letters where needed.

> krista: mark says the springfield chargers are playing vicksburg at the polk
> county events center on friday evening. would you like to go? — oscar
>
> hi, oscar: sure, why don't we meet after english class? Oh, tell mark and maria
> I've got some info on the civil war assignment. — krista

Krista: Mark says the Springfield Chargers are playing Vicksburg at the Polk

County Events Center on Friday evening. Would you like to go? — Oscar

Hi, Oscar: Sure, why don't we meet after English class? Oh, tell Mark and Maria

I've got some info on the Civil War assignment. — Krista

_____

In the Real World

Choose a popular place in your town or a nearby city. Find an interesting visual and write a description of two or three sentences, including at least five proper nouns.

Example   **Union Station** is a popular place to visit in **Kansas City, Missouri.** It is close to **Crown Center** and features **Science City,** an interactive museum.

Answers will vary.

_____

_____

_____

_____

_____

NAME _____   DATE _____

 **LESSON 3** NOUNS # Gender-Specific Nouns

> A **gender-specific** noun is one that indicates the gender (male or female) of a person.
> Common examples include *policeman*, *mankind*, and *waitress*.
>
> Try to avoid such nouns, since they sometimes involve stereotypes or exclude
> women. For example, using the gender-specific noun *policeman* may imply that all law
> enforcement officers are male. Likewise, using *mankind* may seem to exclude women. In
> writing and speaking, use more inclusive nouns, such as *police officer*, *people*, and *waiter*.

Try It Out

The following word search contains eight gender-specific nouns. Complete the word search.
Then, for each gender-specific noun, write an appropriate non-gender-specific noun.

B	U	S	I	N	E	S	S	M	A	N
K	A	N	S	G	I	R	O	T	S	F
S	T	E	W	A	R	D	E	S	S	I
C	H	A	I	R	M	A	N	S	J	R
C	L	E	R	G	Y	M	A	N	U	E
W	A	I	T	R	E	S	S	I	N	M
I	N	A	C	T	R	E	S	S	A	A
E	X	S	P	O	K	E	S	M	A	N

businessperson, flight attendant, chairperson/chair,

minister/priest/rabbi, waiter, actor,

spokesperson/representative, fire fighter

Go Grammar! 5

Taking It Further

View a half-hour cartoon or television show and write a short paragraph on an example of gender stereotyping or gender-specific language.

Example   In a show that I saw, a man kept talking about his wife as the "little woman." He could have just called her his wife or used her proper name.

Answers will vary.

_____

_____

_____

_____

_____

_____

In the Real World

With a partner, write a short humorous skit in which a character becomes offended by the use of gender-specific nouns. Then, rehearse and perform your skit for the class.

Example   Director: You know, you're quite an accomplished actress.
Actor: What did you call me?

Answers will vary.

_____

_____

_____

_____

_____

_____

_____

NAME _____   DATE _____

 **LESSON 4** NOUNS

Concrete and Abstract Nouns

A **concrete noun** names something that can be seen, heard, tasted, felt, or smelled.

Examples   table   classmate   encyclopedia   water

An **abstract noun** names something that cannot be perceived by one of the senses. An abstract noun often names a feeling, idea, or quality.

Examples   happiness   love   equality   confidence

Try It Out

1   Write the nouns below in the correct column.

kindness   backpack   concern   hatred   wood   container
pride   vegetable   pleasure   equality   computer   child

Concrete Nouns	Abstract Nouns
Example child	**Example** concern
container	equality
backpack	kindness
wood	hatred
vegetable	pride
computer	pleasure

2   Under each heading below, list five appropriate abstract nouns.

Behavior/Qualities

optimism

anger, sadness, pity, humor,

despair, generosity

Ideas/Skills

spelling

vocabulary, grammar, punctuation,

narration, humor, drama

Sample answers.

3 Now write a brief sentence about the activities you like doing in class. Circle the concrete nouns and underline the concrete nouns.

_____

_____

Taking It Further

Underline the abstract nouns in the following passage. Then, write a sentence about what one of the abstract nouns means in your life.

> Wei-yan talked about freedom in the story. She was impressed by how the
> main character tried to balance responsibility and loyalty with independence
> and happiness.

_____

_____

In the Real World

Read one of the editorial pieces in the "Letters to the Editor" section of a newspaper. Find five abstract nouns and write them below. Use a dictionary to write a brief definition for each noun.

Example   Dear Editor:
In his article, Guy Rundle accurately describes our American fascination with size. Also worth consideration is the vastness of our appetites.
P. Holcomb

Abstract Nouns	Definitions
1 _____	Answers will vary.
2 _____	
3 _____	
4 _____	
5 _____	

Collective Nouns

Collective nouns name groups of people, animals, or objects. A singular verb follows a collective noun if the noun refers to the group as a whole.

Examples   A **herd** of cows is making its way up the hill.
The **team** are wearing their new uniforms.

Try It Out

Match the common nouns below with the appropriate collective nouns that have been jumbled. Use your dictionary if you are not familiar with some collective nouns.

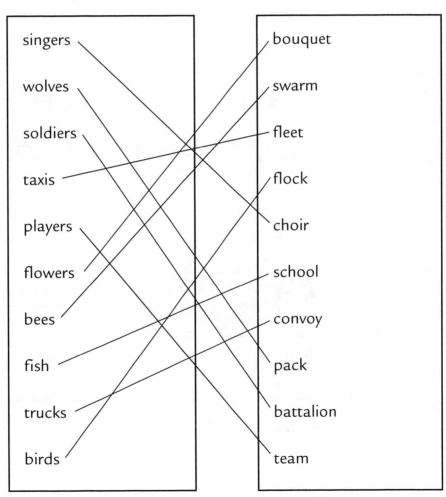

singers

wolves

soldiers

taxis

players

flowers

bees

fish

trucks

birds

bouquet

swarm

fleet

flock

choir

school

convoy

pack

battalion

team

Taking It Further

The following report from a local newspaper has seriously confused some collective nouns!
Rewrite the paragraph so that the underlined collective nouns are in the right places. You can
use a dictionary to check these terms.

A <u>flock</u> of geese scurried past the farmhouse like a <u>gaggle</u> of sheep when a
<u>herd</u> of dogs started barking at a <u>pack</u> of cattle that had wandered out of an
enclosure. Some visiting students had forgotten to close the gate.

A <u>gaggle</u> of geese scurried past the farmhouse like a <u>flock</u> of sheep when a

<u>pack</u> of dogs started barking at a <u>herd</u> of cattle that had wandered out of an

enclosure. Some visiting students had forgotten to close the gate.

In the Real World

Find out to which animals the following collective nouns might refer. You may use a
dictionary to help you.

Collective Noun	Animal
pride	lions
army	ants
swarm	bees, wasps, flies
plague	locusts
pod	whales, dolphins
shoal	fish
sleuth	bears
murder	crows

NAME _____   DATE _____

Personal Pronouns

Pronouns are used in place of nouns. **Personal pronouns** stand for nouns that name people, animals, or things.

Examples **You** can show **us**.
They told **me** to work steadily.

Personal pronouns indicate **person** (first person is the person speaking, second person is the person being spoken to, and third person is the person or thing being spoken about) and **number** (singular or plural).

	Singular		Plural	
	Subject	**Object**	**Subject**	**Object**
1st Person	I	me	we	us
2nd Person	you	you	you	you
3rd Person	he/she/it	him/her/it	they	them

Try It Out

1 Circle the pronouns in each sentence.

   a We like going camping, but they don't.

   b He thought he had caught the trout, but it got away.

   c "You will have to ride together to school," Ms. Lin told them.

   d Leo took us to the museum on Saturday. We had never visited it before.

   e Dan stood up, and then he looked at her in dismay and ran off.

2 Now write a noun to which each pronoun might refer in the sentences above. The first one has been done for you.

a   **We = our family; they = some other people**

b   he = the fisherman; it = the trout

c   you = a group of students; them = the same people

d   us = the speaker and some others; We = the same people; it = the museum

e   he = Dan; her = a girl

Taking It Further

Circle all the personal pronouns in the following passage. Then, write down each pronoun and specify its person and number. The first one is completed for you.

"(I) can't go yet. This foot feels as if (it's) turned into a cabbage. (They) won't like hearing that (I) tripped on the sprinkler and accidentally broke the nozzle! Can all of (you) wait a while?"

Example   I: 1st person singular

it: 3rd person singular; they: 3rd person plural; you: 2nd person plural

In the Real World

Rewrite the following school rule by replacing nouns with pronouns. Write the first sentence in the first person plural and the second sentence in the first person singular.

All students have the right to be free from bullying. Students have a right to seek assistance as soon as they feel threatened.

We have the right to be free from bullying. I have a right to seek assistance

as soon as I feel threatened.

 **LESSON 7 PRONOUNS**

Subject, Object, and Possessive Pronouns

The **subject** (or focus) of a sentence is always a noun or pronoun. You can find the subject by asking "Who?" or "What?" about the verb.

Example **She** is nice.
Ask: "Who is?" Answer: She
She is the subject.

The **object** of a verb is the person or thing upon which the verb acts. The object of a preposition is the noun that follows it. Find the object by asking "Whom?" or "What?" about the verb or preposition.

Example Please save a **seat** for **her**.
Ask: "Save what?" Answer: seat
Ask: "For whom?" Answer: her
Seat is the object of *save. Her* is the object of *for.*

A **possessive pronoun** refers to something that belongs to somebody.

Example My teacher returned **mine** yesterday.

	Subject	Object	Possessive
1st Person	I (sing.)	me (sing.)	mine (sing.)
	we (pl.)	us (pl.)	ours (pl.)
2nd Person	you (sing. & pl.)	you (sing. & pl.)	yours (sing. & pl.)
3rd Person	he/she/it (sing.)	him/her/it (sing.)	his/hers/its (sing.)
	they (pl.)	them (pl.)	theirs (pl.)

Try It Out

Decide whether each underlined pronoun is *subject, object,* or *possessive.*

1 The teacher welcomed <u>me</u> to the school. ___*object*_____

2 After reading fantasy novels, <u>we</u> discuss <u>them</u> in class. ___*subject, object*___

3 That ball is <u>ours</u>. Give <u>it</u> back! _possessive, object_

4 When <u>she</u> found out she had won, <u>we</u> all cheered. _subject, subject_

5 <u>She</u> said it was <u>theirs</u>; I don't believe <u>her</u>. _subject, possessive, object_

6 Why do <u>you</u> think the teacher gave it to <u>you</u>? _subject, object_

Taking It Further

Check the sentences that include the correct personal pronouns. Circle any incorrect pronouns, and write the correct ones on the line provided. Remember to put yourself second, after the other person, in writing and speech.

1 Jan and ⬚me⬚ play in the same volleyball team. _I_

2 Paul said he and they were going to audition for the play. ✔

3 Ms. Cantú gave ⬚me and my sister⬚ a delicious mango. _my sister and me_

4 I asked Dad if ⬚me and him⬚ could go fishing next weekend. _he and I_

5 Tell Jean to ride between you and me. ✔

6 The reward was given to Martin and ⬚I⬚. _me_

In the Real World

Find a personal pronoun in a newspaper headline and write the headline below.

Example

Answers will vary.

President: I won't budge!

 **LESSON 8** PRONOUNS

Gender-Specific Personal Pronouns

The gender of personal pronouns sometimes causes problems. In the past, if the gender of a noun was unknown, a masculine pronoun (*he/him/his*) was used. Now, you should avoid such pronoun usage and, instead, use pronouns that do not exclude one sex or the other.

However, avoiding the problem can be difficult. For example, the sentence below requires a singular pronoun (such as *he*). Of course, *he* is gender-specific.

> **Example** If a student has poor study habits, _____ should seek help.

i One option is to revise the sentence and use a third-person plural pronoun (*they/them*). These pronouns do not distinguish the gender of the noun.

> **Example** If **students** have poor study habits, **they** should seek help.

ii Another option is to use the combination *he or she*.

> **Example** If a student has poor study habits, **he or she** should seek help.

Try It Out

Rewrite the following passage in the third-person plural to avoid gender-specific pronouns.

> A teacher works hard to inspire learning and self-confidence in his students. When a student is having trouble with her work, a teacher can help her become organized, manage time, and stay motivated.

Teachers work hard to inspire learning and self-confidence in their students.

When students are having trouble with their work, teachers can help them

become organized, manage time, and stay motivated.

_____

Taking It Further

Change each of the following gender-specific sentences by using either a third-person plural pronoun (they/them) or the combination *he or she/him or her.*

1 A doctor does his best to help patients.

   Doctors do their best to help patients.

   Answers may vary.

2 A truck driver enjoys a good laugh when he takes a break.

   A truck driver enjoys a good laugh when he or she takes a break.

3 Does a secretary receive appreciation for her work?

   Do secretaries receive appreciation for their work?

4 Call an electrician and explain the problem to him.

   Call an electrician and explain the problem to him or her.

5 A kindergarten teacher needs to be friendly but firm with her students.

   Kindergarten teachers need to be friendly but firm with their students.

6 A trial lawyer spends most of his day in court.

   Trial lawyers spend most of their day in court.

7 A good bus driver will help passengers when he reaches a stop.

   A good bus driver will help passengers when he or she reaches a stop.

8 When a nurse is on duty, many people may need her urgently.

   When a nurse is on duty, many people may need him or her urgently.

In the Real World

Write a brief description of the qualities you most admire in a person, using non-gender specific pronouns.

Example My ideal friend has a sparkling sense of humor. He or she helps others without thinking . . .

Answers will vary.

_____

_____

_____

_____

LESSON 9 Action Verbs
VERBS

> Action **verbs** are doing words. They describe physical or mental actions.
>
> **Examples** Maria **combed** her long, black hair. (physical action)
> Roger **worried** about his grades. (mental action)

Try It Out

See how many action verbs you can make using only
the letters in the grid. You may use a letter only once in
each word.

Answers may vary.

L	S	O	E
I	P	A	K
G	R	B	M
V	Y	T	C

grip, live, lock, lose, rip, take, grab, move, pay, lop, tick,

pack, soak, tack

Taking It Further

In the sentences below, remove each underlined *be* verb and the common noun that
follows it. Then, replace the words you removed with an action verb. The first one has been
done for you.

1 Theo and Jackie <u>are</u> the winners of the writing competition.

   Theo and Jackie won the writing competition.

2 Those players <u>were</u> losers in the tournament.

   Those players lost the tournament.

3 Nina <u>will be</u> on vacation in South Dakota.

   Nina will vacation in South Dakota.

4 They <u>were</u> builders of affordable houses.

   They built affordable houses.

5 Some students <u>were</u> participants in the fun run.

   Some students participated in the fun run.

6 They <u>were</u> helpers for a day.

They helped for a day.

7 She <u>was</u> the painter of our classroom.

She painted our classroom.

8 I <u>am</u> a success when I stay focused.

I succeed when I stay focused.

In the Real World

Write a brief set of numbered instructions on how to plant a tree, make a mask, or clean a pet or a car. Start each numbered instruction with an action verb.

Example

How to brush your teeth

1. Squeeze toothpaste onto your brush.

2. Wet the toothpaste and brush with water.

3. Hold the toothbrush handle firmly.

4. Put the toothbrush . . .

Answers will vary.

How to _____

_____

_____

_____

_____

_____

_____

_____

LESSON 10 — VERBS — # The Verb *Be*

The verb *be* shows what a person or thing is (present), was (past), or will be (future).

Examples Jeremy **is** in my homeroom.
The apple **was** bruised.
The city **will be** crowded.

		Singular	**Plural**
Present Tense	1st Person	I am	we are
	2nd Person	you are	you are
	3rd Person	he/she/it is	they are
Past Tense	1st Person	I was	we were
	2nd Person	you were	you were
	3rd Person	he/she/it was	they were
Future Tense	1st Person	I will be	we will be
	2nd Person	you will be	you will be
	3rd Person	he/she/it will be	they will be

These terms are very useful when learning another language.

Try It Out

Insert the appropriate tense (past/present/future) of the verb *be* in the spaces.

Answers may vary.

"I __am__ not happy," said Mrs Carbuncle, who __was__ grumpy by nature. "That __was__ very naughty of you, Tom. Your mother __will be__ very disappointed when she hears."

It __was__ the end of the semester and the students __were__ restless.

"I know that you __are__ tired of school, but next week __is/will be__ spring break," said Mr. Young. "Let's finish this work so that you __will be__ free to enjoy yourselves. Now where __were__ we?"

Taking It Further

Write three sentences about an out-of-the-ordinary animal or person. Include an appropriate form of the verb *be* at least three times and underline each one. Choose one of the following opening sentences.

Answers will vary.

- Our surprise visitor was a _____.
- I can see it coming closer now!

_____

_____

_____

_____

_____

_____

In the Real World

Congratulations on making the finals of the Great Being Verbs Competition! As you know, the person who can place the most *be* verbs in a single sentence that makes sense will be world champion. Sharpen your pencils — you have two minutes . . .

Example   It is wonderful when you are with someone who you know will be a true friend.

Answers will vary.

_____

_____

_____

_____

LESSON 11 **VERBS** # Verb Tenses

The tense of a verb tells the time of the action shown by the verb. We have three main tenses: past, present, and future.

Examples I now **live** in East St. Louis. (present)
I **lived** in Indonesia as a small child. (past)
I **will live** in the Bahamas when I'm a millionaire. (future)

Most verbs form the past tense by adding *-ed*. You may have noticed that some verbs form the past tense in other ways. These verbs are irregular.

Example I normally **eat** cereal for breakfast.
Last night I **ate** a whole watermelon.

Your dictionary provides the forms of irregular verbs.

Try It Out

1 Complete the table with the correct tenses of the verbs.

	Present	**Past**	**Future**
seem	seem	seemed	will seem
become	become	became	will become
work	work	worked	will work
play	play	played	will play
study	study	studied	will study
lose	lose	lost	will lose
drink	drink	drank	will drink
go	go	went	will go

2 Circle each verb and write its tense.

a My dad (walks) to work most days. _present_____

b Tara and I (swam) one mile during training yesterday. _past_____

c After all that practice, the school band (will sound) outstanding at the concert. ____future____

d Dan (wrote) only ten lines for his essay. ___past___

e I (waited) for you at the school entrance for a very long time. ___past___

f He (ll fix) my bike over the weekend. ___future___

g He (travels) all over the place to look for rare plants. ___present___

h While you (look) for her in the kitchen, I (ll look) upstairs. ___present, future___

Taking It Further

Complete the sentences. Try to use interesting verbs. You may not use the verb *be*. Then circle
each verb you used.

> Sample answers.

1 Yesterday at school, we (ran) five laps in gym class.

2 Tomorrow afternoon, Mom (will buy) me a new basketball.

3 Usually on weekends, I (ride) my bike along the bike path.

4 Last night on TV, I (saw) a program about volcanoes.

5 Every morning before school, I (make) my lunch.

6 Next week after school, (I'll attend) my first track meet.

7 Last winter break, we (visited) my aunt in Seattle.

8 When I have saved fifty dollars, (I'll buy) a portable CD player.

In the Real World

The tenses in this news report are mixed up. Rewrite it completely in the past tense.

> Yesterday, dozens of hot air balloons take to the skies and floated over the city.
> Balloonists from all over the world are delighted by the perfect weather and
> will promise to return next year.

Yesterday, dozens of hot air balloons took to the skies and floated over the
city. Balloonists from all over the world were delighted by the perfect weather
and promised to return next year.

LESSON 12 Verb Phrases
VERBS

A **verb phrase** includes a helping verb that is followed by a main verb. The main verb may be in the form of a participle. A present participle ends in *-ing*. A past participle for regular verbs ends in *-ed*.

Example   The gardener **was working** very hard.
The champion **has played** here many times.

The most common helping verbs are *am, is, are, was, were* (followed by a present participle) and *have, has, had* (followed by a past participle).

Try It Out

Complete the table by adding the missing participles. Helping verbs have been included in parentheses to help you. One regular and one irregular verb have been done for you.

Note that irregular verbs form their past participles differently. Use your dictionary if you need help.

Present	Present Participle	Past Participle
talk	(is) **talking**	(has) **talked**
bite	(are) **biting**	(have) **bitten**
clean	(was) cleaning	(had) cleaned
fill	(were) filling	(have) filled
try	(are) trying	(have) tried
do	(is) doing	(has) done
eat	(am) eating	(had) eaten
go	(is) going	(has) gone
do	(was) doing	(has) done
think	(am) thinking	(had) thought

Go Grammar!   23

Taking It Further

Complete the sentences by adding a helping verb and a participle. | Answers may vary. |

1 Yesterday I (do) __was doing__ my homework when the fire alarm went off.

2 I (finish) __have finished__ all my assignments for this week.

3 Next weekend, we (go) __are going__ camping.

4 The teacher said that I (work) __had worked__ hard on my assignment.

5 Sam (brush) __is brushing/has brushed__ his teeth extra well because he is going to the dentist.

6 The Patels (put) __have put/are putting__ their house up for sale.

7 My cousin (arrive) __had arrived__ home before I appeared.

8 Ella (have) __has had__ that bike for so long that she (grow) __has grown__ out of it.

In the Real World

Choose either a page from a book you like reading or a magazine article. Find and list at least five verb phrases. Then, identify the participle in each phrase as either present or past.

| Answers will vary. |

_____

_____

_____

_____

_____

 **LESSON 13** VERBS

Verbs in Indirect Speech

Direct speech represents the actual words spoken by a speaker. When someone else reports what is said, the words are **indirect speech.** Indirect speech requires changes in person and tense.

Example **Direct Speech**   Mia said, "I'm going to join the choir."
              Indirect Speech Mia said that **she is going** to join the choir.

Try It Out

Rewrite these sentences as indirect speech.

Example   Enrico said, "I want to visit Panama to see my relatives."

Enrico said he wants to visit Panama to see his relatives.

1 Martha said, "I do the difficult homework first."

   Martha said that she does the difficult homework first.

2 "Would you like to come to my place to watch the playoffs?" Tim asked Caleb.

   Tim asked Caleb if he would like to come to his place to watch the playoffs.

3 "How long will you be touring Europe?" the reporter asked Cindy.

   The reporter asked Cindy how long she would be touring Europe.

4 "Independence Day has become the most important US national holiday," declared the history teacher.

   The history teacher declared that Independence Day has become the most
   important US national holiday.

5 The Hollywood producer told the actor, "I want to make you a star."

   The Hollywood producer told the actor that he (OR she) wanted to make her
   (OR him) a star.

Taking It Further

Rewrite the following dialogue as indirect speech.
To create variety, use verbs from the following list: *demanded, complained, explained,* and *informed.*

"Why does Stephanie always get to play on offense?" Jill asked her basketball coach in a frustrated tone.

"Stephanie is tall and a proven scorer," explained Coach Carol.

"But Stephanie is the only player who misses practice, so why should she get the glory?"

"Actually, Stephanie volunteered to play defense this game because she thought you would enjoy the opportunity. As for missing practice, Stephanie has to train with her neighborhood team since she happens to be captain."

Jill asked her basketball coach why Stephanie always

| Answers may vary. |

gets to play on offense. Coach Carol explained that Stephanie is tall and a

proven scorer. Jill complained about Stephanie missing practice yet getting

the glory. Coach Carol informed Jill that Stephanie actually volunteered to

play on defense this game because she thought Jill would enjoy the opportu-

nity. Stephanie has to miss practice because she happens to be captain of her

neighborhood team and so has to train with them.

In the Real World

Recall a recent conversation you overheard between two people or between yourself and a friend. In your notebook, write the conversation in indirect speech. Try using a range of verbs to describe how the words were said.

LESSON 14 ADJECTIVES

Adjectives

An adjective is a word that describes a noun or pronoun.

Examples A **big** cat is in my yard. (The adjective *big* describes *cat*.)
They are **thirsty**. (The adjective *thirsty* describes *They*.)

Try It Out

Circle the adjectives in each sentence.

1   The students had a (fun) time at the (old) fortress.

2   Teachers should encourage (young) students to take (regular) breaks when they are doing homework.

3   The players need to be more (careful) when they play softball near windows.

4   It's a (good) idea to add (rotted) compost to the soil before you plant the (new) seedlings.

5   When we visited the (elderly) man to fix his fence, he said that we were very (kind).

6   She thinks she's (brilliant) just because she got a (gold) star in art.

7   I used an (old) racquet that was too (heavy) for me.

8   As the (slimy) creature slowly crawled out of a (damp) hole, the (frightened) child ran for help.

Taking It Further

These words are also considered adjectives: *this/that, these/those, my/our, your, his/her/its, their.*
Circle all the adjectives in the following description.

(This) car was an (amazing) combination of (different) (old) parts. Only (its) (flashy) hubcaps were the (latest) style. The rest of it looked like a (rolling) museum of (ancient) (automotive) history.

Even more ⬡surprising⬡ was the ⬡remarkable⬡ person who stepped out of it. His clothes, like the car, came from ⬡various⬡ places and times. He wore a ⬡leather⬡ boot on ⬡one⬡ foot and a ⬡fancy⬡ slipper on the other. Over ⬡short⬡ pants and stockings hung an ⬡armored⬡ skirt like those worn by ⬡Roman⬡ soldiers. A ⬡heavy⬡ cape covered his ⬡orange⬡ sweater, and he wore a ⬡battered⬡ crown over a ⬡broad⬡ sombrero.

In the Real World

1 Copy a recipe and circle all the adjectives, including adjectives of quantity and number.

Example

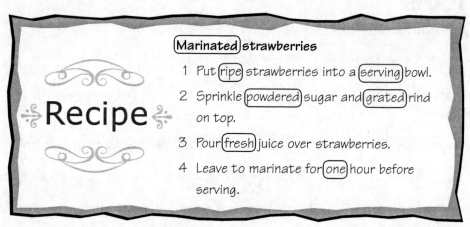

Recipe

⬡Marinated⬡ strawberries

1 Put ⬡ripe⬡ strawberries into a ⬡serving⬡ bowl.

2 Sprinkle ⬡powdered⬡ sugar and ⬡grated⬡ rind on top.

3 Pour ⬡fresh⬡ juice over strawberries.

4 Leave to marinate for ⬡one⬡ hour before serving.

Answers will vary.

_____

_____

_____

_____

2 Now imagine you have a home remedy or kitchen science experiment to make. Write your recipe below and use at least four adjectives.

Example   Put ⬡four⬡ drops of ⬡hot⬡ sauce in a glass of ⬡fresh⬡ vinegar . . .

Answers will vary.

_____

_____

_____

_____

LESSON (15) Comparison of Adjectives
ADJECTIVES

> You can compare two or more nouns by using special adjective forms. The **comparative form** (ending in *-er*) compares two nouns, and the **superlative form** (ending in *-est*) compares three or more nouns.
>
> **Examples** I am **smaller** than my best friend. (comparative)
> You are the **smallest** in the class. (superlative)
>
> Some adjectives form the comparative by adding *more* and the superlative by adding *most*.
>
> I am **more athletic** than Greg, but Gina is **most athletic.**

Try It Out

1 Ask five classmates the questions below and record your answers on the table provided.

	Students				
	1	2	3	4	5
How tall are you?					
When is your birthday?					

2 Now answer the following items in complete sentences, and circle the comparative or superlative adjectives that you use.

   a Who is the tallest in the group?   Answers will vary.

   _____

   b Who is the shortest?

   _____

   c Write a sentence comparing the height of two students.

   _____

   d Who is the oldest in the group?

   _____

   e Who is the youngest?

   _____

   f Write a sentence comparing the age of two students.

   _____

Taking It Further

Here are some common exceptions to the standard comparative and superlative forms of adjectives.

Adjective	Comparative	Superlative
good	better	best
bad	worse	worst
many	more	most
much/some	more	most
little	less	least

Use the table to choose the appropriate form of the adjective in each of the following sentences.

1   I'm pleased that my breaststroke is getting (good) __better__ .

2   My cold was bad yesterday and, unfortunately, it is (bad) __worse__ today.

3   Our class raised the (little) __least__ money for the school, so we felt terrible.

4   The teacher said I'm too loud and should make (little) __less__ noise in class.

5   Cathy got one hundred percent—her (good) __best__ test score ever.

6   She gave the (much) __most__ effort to her class presentation.

7   Emma has (many) __more__ books in her bag than I have. It must weigh a ton!

8   The (bad) __worst__ thing about listening to the radio is that the tunes stay in my head and I can't get rid of them.

In the Real World

If you were given the choice to be a pop star, professional athlete, or adventurer, which career would you choose? Explain your choice and include at least two comparative adjectives and two superlative adjectives. You may want to use some adjectives from the box.

interesting   challenging   dangerous   tiring   famous   unusual

Answers will vary.

_____

_____

Adverbs

LESSON **16**
ADVERBS

Adverbs are used to tell more about a verb, an adjective, or another adverb. Adverbs often tell how, why, when, or where something happens.

Example Susie danced **gracefully** all evening. (The adverb *gracefully* tells how Susie danced.)

Adverbs are often formed by adding -ly to an adjective, as in *slow**ly**, quick**ly**, helpful**ly**.* However, there are exceptions, such as the following adverbs.

The music was **too** loud.
She is **very** happy with the result.
He **almost** cried when he heard the news.

Try It Out

1   Change the following adjectives into adverbs.

quick   strong   wise   brave   horrible   happy   weary   true

quickly, strongly, wisely, bravely, horribly, happily, wearily, truly

2   Circle the adverbs in each of the following sentences.

a   Jackson whistled cheerfully as he mowed the lawn.

b   I nearly fainted when he signed an autograph for me.

c   The champion played poorly in the game.

d   I dislike the trip on the bus; it takes so long.

e   Gently the girl reached under the bed and searched eagerly for her present.

f   I'm too tired to practice tonight.

g   The teacher smiled broadly while the class chatted noisily.

h   I'm not old enough to drive a car.

Taking It Further

Some adverbs tell us when something happened (such as *yesterday, soon*) or how often something happens (*always, sometimes, usually, often*).

Complete the following sentences with an appropriate adverb.

Sample answers.

Please note: Some are regular -ly adverbs, but others are not!

1   The whole team played very __well/badly__.

2   I'm not feeling __well__. It must be something I ate.

3   __Sometimes/Often__ after school, I go to a friend's house.

4   Whenever I do this card trick, someone __usually__ ruins it.

5   He __reluctantly/happily__ accepted the gift.

6   At lunchtime I __always/usually__ hang around with my friends.

7   The beach was __so__ crowded that there was hardly room for our towels.

8   He must not have cooked the potatoes long __enough__ because they were __too__ hard.

In the Real World

Think of a product and make up an advertisement for it in the space below. Your product could be a shampoo, clothing, a wonder vitamin, or a new food item. Use at least four adverbs. Make your advertisement colorful and catchy. The example below might give you some ideas.

NAME _____   DATE _____

Conjunctions: *And, But, Because*

> **Conjunctions** join words and groups of words within a sentence. They can also be used to connect sentences.
>
> **Examples** A balance of work **and** play is essential for a healthy life.
> I went home early **because** I felt sick.

Try It Out

Choose from the conjunctions *and, but,* and *because* to complete the sentences.

1   We bought apples ____*and*____ oranges for a fruit punch.

2   Glen arrives early at school ____*because*____ his mother drops him off on her way to work.

3   I like going out, ____*but*____ staying home is also relaxing.

4   We had four different cereals ____*but*____ no milk!

5   I suppose you enjoy reading ____*because*____ it puts you in another world.

6   Fluffy bolted across the road ____*and*____ up a tree.

7   You can go with Brad, ____*but*____ please finish folding the towels first.

8   I tried again ____*and*____ again, ____*but*____ I failed to get onto the team ____*because*____ I still needed a little more training.

Taking It Further

Use a conjunction to join the sentences and make one sentence.

1   Kim's group made their own costumes. They also made their own props.

   Kim's group made their own costumes and props. | Answers may vary. |

2   We went shopping. We had run out of bread and milk.

   We went shopping because we had run out of bread and milk.

3   I need to take the subway. I don't have my bike.

   I need to take the subway because I don't have my bike.

4 I had hoped to see them. They had already gone by the time I arrived.

I had hoped to see them, but they had already gone by the time I arrived.

5 The windows and curtains were all closed. There was a heat wave.

The windows and curtains were all closed because there was a heat wave.

6 The swimmer stood on the diving board. She looked around at the cheering crowd.

The swimmer stood on the diving board and looked around at the cheering crowd.

7 I could not go to the movies. I had to look after my little brother and sister.

I could not go to the movies because I had to look after my little brother and sister.

8 The woman stood there with her eyes closed. Her mouth was wide open.

The woman stood there with her eyes closed and her mouth wide open.

In the Real World

Read the following passage from An Na's *A Step From Heaven*. Rewrite it in longer sentences using *and* and *but*. How does connecting sentences change the passage?

Example   Go to the edge, Young Ju, but only put your feet in . . .

Just to the edge, Young Ju. Only your feet. Stay there.
Cold. Cold water. Oh. My toes are fish. Come here. Fast. Look.
What is it, Young Ju?
See my toes. See how they are swimming in the sea? Like fish.
Yes, they are little fat piggy fish.
Ahhh! Tickles.
Come on. Up. Keep your legs around me. Are you ready to go swim in the waves?
Hold me. Hold me.

Answers will vary.

 **More Conjunctions**

CONJUNCTIONS

Conjunctions (words that "join together") connect individual words or groups of words.

There are two categories of conjunctions.

i Conjunctions can join individual words that are the same part of speech. The most often used conjunctions of this kind are *so, but, and, yet,* and *or.*

Examples Nouns: Hockey is played with a *stick* **and** *puck.*
Verbs: I *run* **and** *lift* weights once a week.
Adjectives: She was *gentle* **but** *firm.*
Pronouns: Is that cake for *her* **or** *me?*
Adverbs: Ian thanked Lucy *quietly* **yet** *sincerely.*

They can also connect groups of words.

Examples The performers arrived late, **so** the crowd was disappointed.
Are children permitted to stand, **or** must they remain seated?

ii Certain conjunctions can join one group of words that cannot stand alone without the other. Common conjunctions that do so are *because, whenever, until, once, wherever, since, unless, after, before, when, while, if, although, where,* and *whether.*

Examples I will follow **wherever** he leads.
Don't look back **once** you have decided.

Try It Out

Use a conjunction to complete these sentences.

Answers may vary.

1 The students looked nervous __but__ determined.

2 Dollars __and__ cents are currency.

3 Would you like to stop for a drink of water __or__ keep working?

4 Majid should practice the violin __before/until__ he has his lesson.

5 The coach spoke angrily __yet/but__ sensibly.

6 Keep your seat belts fastened __until__ the plane has stopped.

7 __After__ we finished dinner, we went for a walk along the beach.

8 Tom said that he will take care of the cat __while__ we are away.

Taking It Further

1   Circle the words that are joined by the conjunctions shown in bold. Then, either write
    their parts of speech or state that they are "groups of words."

   Example   They talked [softly] **but** [quickly]. ___adverbs___

   a   The dog [barked] **and** [whined]. ___verbs___

   b   The house was [small] **but** [welcoming]. ___adjectives___

   c   Will you have [salad] **or** [fruit]? ___nouns___

   d   The singer played guitar [simply] **but** [well]. ___adverbs___

   e   [I was hungry,] **but** [I didn't want to eat junk food.] ___groups of words___

   f   The rolls are for [you] **and** [me]. ___pronouns___

   g   [You have to go to Grandma's afternoon tea] **unless** [she says otherwise.] ___groups of words___

   h   **Whenever** [we go camping] [the weather is awful.] ___groups of words___

2   Complete this advertisement with appropriate conjunctions.

   Great savings, ___but___ hurry ___while___ supplies last!

   Choose from our deluxe stove ___or___ standard-model electric mixers.

In the Real World

Write five sentences describing your biggest dream. Include at least four appropriate
conjunctions.

   Example   I want to discover a new species because my discovery would add
                 to our knowledge of animals.

   > Answers will vary.

_____

_____

_____

_____

LESSON 19 Common Prepositions
PREPOSITIONS

Prepositions connect nouns or pronouns to other words. Some common prepositions are listed below.

of	to	in	for
from	with	on	at
by	between	up	above
under	among	over	across
after	down	through	before

Try It Out

1 Complete each sentence with an appropriate preposition.

Answers may vary.

a The water __in__ the pool was freezing.

b Will this picture fade __over__ the years?

c New York differs greatly __from__ Calcutta.

d Streaks of rain ran __down__ the windshield.

e I usually go __to__ bed __at__ nine o'clock.

f I last saw the old gentleman standing __beside__ the library.

g Stephie prefers snow skiing __to__ water skiing.

h Mom shares things equally __between__ my brother and me.

i The dog escaped by digging __under__ the fence.

j Did you know that someone has rowed all the way __across__ the Atlantic Ocean?

2 Underline all the prepositions in the car review below.

After a test drive, I was soundly impressed by the new model. The car will be offered with four sets of options, from basic and mid-level to luxury and sporty. It has also undergone improvements in the braking system and suspension.

Go Grammar! (37)

Taking It Further

Finish these sentences by adding one or more prepositions and other words.

Example   The old man went <u>into the shop and bought a newspaper.</u>

1   We traveled <u>to Utah by train.</u>

Sample answers.

2   They went <u>to the top of the Sears Tower.</u>

3   I looked <u>deep into the well but saw no bottom.</u>

4   The burglar struggled <u>with the guard before giving up.</u>

5   The wizard appeared <u>in a cloud of sparkling confetti.</u>

6   The family ate dinner <u>around the dining room table.</u>

7   The eagle soared <u>above the wave tops, looking for food.</u>

8   The author spoke <u>to a room packed with excited fans.</u>

In the Real World

Find a piece of written text — a passage from a novel, a news report, song lyrics, or a magazine article. Rewrite it below without prepositions, leaving a space for each one. Then swap texts with a partner and see if you can replace the prepositions correctly.

Example   "It's easy," said Gillian. "We go _____ here, _____ this

bridge, and then _____ the overhanging tree branch."

Answers will vary.

_____

_____

_____

_____

_____

_____

_____

LESSON 20 PREFIXES **Negative Prefixes**

> **Prefixes** are word parts that are placed before other words or word parts to change the meaning. **Negative prefixes** change the meaning of a word to its opposite.
>
> **Example** **non**sense **de**flate **dis**agree **mis**understand
> **un**natural **anti**theft

Try It Out

Write the missing negative prefix. Choose from the following: *de-, dis-, non-, un-, mis-*.

1 Do you have _non_fat milk?

2 Not checking the facts before printing the article was so _un_professional.

3 They had a huge _dis_agreement and now they're not talking to each other.

4 The senator said it was _un-_American to limit free speech.

5 Shelley flooded the kitchen when she _de_frosted the freezer.

6 Nathan was annoyed by the _mis_spellings in my paper.

7 After he successfully _de_fused the bomb, the soldier stood shaking.

8 Our neighbor's dog is very _dis_obedient. It rarely comes when it's called.

Taking It Further

1 Team up with a classmate and find five words for each prefix.
Use a dictionary if needed.   Sample answers.

a non- _nonbeing, noncentral, nonfiction, nonglare, nonjudgmental_

b de- _decelerate, declassify, decline, decrease, descend_

c dis- _disappear, disclaim, dishonest, displace, displease_

d anti- _antiaircraft, antifreeze, antihero, antiviral, antiwar_

e mis- _misalign, misbehave, misdiagnose, misfire, misquote_

f in- _incapable, incoherent, incompatible, indigestion, inefficient_

g un- _unable, unclear, unhappy, unpopular, unsafe_

h im- _immature, immoral, immortal, impatient, impersonal_

2 Change the following words by adding a prefix to mean "not."

a cooperative _uncooperative/noncooperative_

b sensitive _insensitive/nonsensitive_

c friendly _unfriendly_

d probable _improbable_

e represent _misrepresent_

f bacterial _antibacterial/nonbacterial_

g regulate _deregulate_

h comfort _discomfort_

In the Real World

Create three newspaper headlines about a recent news event or a personal interest such as a favorite sport. Then rewrite the headlines with negative prefixes.

Example   **With negative prefix:**

Jackson happy with soccer win   Jackson unhappy with soccer win

LESSON 21 **PREFIXES** # More Prefixes

> **Prefixes** are word parts that are placed before other words or word parts to change the meaning.
>
> **Examples** **hyper**active   *hyper-* = especially, excessively
> **super**natural   *super-* = above, more than, very
> **sub**marine   *sub-* = under, less than, part of
> **re**visit   *re-* = again

Try It Out

For each phrase below, add an appropriate prefix from the list above to indicate the same meaning in one word.

1 very sensitive ___hypersensitive___

2 gain again ___regain___

3 below standard ___substandard___

4 more than human ___superhuman___

5 united again ___reunited___

6 very successful star (celebrity) ___superstar___

7 too active ___hyperactive___

8 part of a continent ___subcontinent___

Taking It Further

1 Create a new word with the indicated meaning by adding a prefix to each root word below.

a to bring to mind again (v.) __re__ member

b push below the surface (v.) __sub__ merge

c a second tally of a vote (n.) __re__ count

d be in charge of someone (v.) __super__ vise

e finding too many faults (adj.) __hyper__ critical

2 Here are some more prefixes.

tele- = distant	*bi-* = two
semi- = half, part	*micro-* = small, minute
trans- = across, change	*pre-* = before

Write down four words that contain each prefix. Use a dictionary if you wish.

telephone, telemarketing, telepathy, television, telescope;   Sample answers.

bimonthly, bivalve, bilateral, biennial, bifocal, binoculars;

semicolon, semiconscious, semidetached, semifinal,

semiprofessional, semiprecious;

microbiology, microchip, microphone, microscope, microtechnology;

transaction, translation, transmit, transparent, transport;

predict, prepare, presume, prevent, preview

In the Real World

Make a list of words relating to science and communication that contain the prefixes covered on this worksheet. You should be able to find at least ten words. Use a dictionary if you wish.

Example   microchip

hyperfine, hyperparasite, hyperspace; supercluster,   Sample answers.

superfluid, supersonic; subatomic, subduction, sublimate; reaction, reactor,

retransmit; telecommunications, telegraph, television, telescope; bilayer,

bimolecular, bivalve; semiconductor, semiliquid, semisolid; microbiology,

microchip, microphone, microscope, microtechnology; transmit, transmission;

precursor, prescientific, preview

LESSON (22) **Common Suffixes**
PREFIXES

> **Suffixes** are word parts that are placed at the ends of other words. A suffix can change a word's meaning and part of speech.
>
> **Example** *beauty* (noun) + *-ful* becomes *beautiful* (adjective)
>
> Common suffixes to make adjectives include: *-less, -ful, -ous, -able, -ible, -ly.*
> Common suffixes to make nouns include: *-ment, -hood, -ness, -tion, -ship, -ism.*

Try It Out

1   Add a suffix to make the words in parentheses into adjectives.

   a   The story was (wonder) __wonderful__ .

   b   That dog is so (friend) __friendly__ ; it likes wagging its tail.

   c   You need to be (care) __careful__ when lighting a campfire.

   d   That website says so little that it's (use) __useless__ .

   e   If Kevin said he'd do it, then he will. He's (depend) __dependable__ .

   f   There are many (poison) __poisonous__ creatures in the jungle.

   g   The value of these dolls makes them quite (collect) __collectible__ .

   h   (Mountain) __Mountainous__ waves surged during the storm.

   i   If the alarm sounds, walk to the front gate in an (order) __orderly__ fashion.

   j   The painters were (care) __careless__ and spilled paint on the floor.

2   Underline the suffixes in the following advertisement for a mountain lodge. Use your dictionary if required.

> Relax in sheer content<u>ment</u> on the porch as you listen to the melodi<u>ous</u> songs of birds. Experience the delight<u>ful</u> companion<u>ship</u> of your fellow guests in a taste<u>ful</u> environ<u>ment</u>.

Taking It Further

1 Make these words into nouns by adding a suffix. You may use your dictionary.

concentrate	entertain	pollute	friend
happy	child	critic	suggest

concentration, entertainment, pollution, friendship,

> Answers may vary.

happiness, childhood, criticism, suggestion

2 Change these nouns into adjectives by using suffixes.

hope	marvel	dread	love
honor	week	wire	moment

hopeful/hopeless, marvelous, dreadful, lovely,

> Answers may vary.

honorable, weekly, wireless, momentous

In the Real World

This passage contains incorrect suffixes. Rewrite it correctly. Use a dictionary if you wish.

> Films provide wonderable escapement for the audience. Herohood and relationisms are very popular themes. Some audiences gain a lot of enjoyship from watching fameful actors in "buddy" films, showing courageousity and friendhood. Others like to see a character overcome difficulties with determinism and patience.

Films provide wonderful escapism for the audience. Heroism and relationships

are very popular themes. Some audiences gain a lot of enjoyment from

watching famous actors in "buddy" films, showing courageousness and friend-

ship. Others like to see a character overcome difficulties with

determination and patience.

(LESSON 23) Apostrophes in Contractions
PUNCTUATION

> The **apostrophe** can be used to indicate that one or more letters have been left out of a word. Shortening a word creates a **contraction**.
>
> **Examples** **It's** wise to try your best at any task. (It's = It is)
> **You're** well prepared for the test. (You're = You are)

Try It Out

1 Write the contracted form.

it is	it's
does not	doesn't
they are	they're
were not	weren't
you are	you're
cannot	can't
I will	I'll
let us	let's
we have	we've
I am	I'm

2 Write out the contractions in full.

didn't	did not
couldn't	could not
she'll	she will
I'd	I had/I would
he's	he is/he has
aren't	are not
there's	there is/there has
isn't	is not
could've	could have
won't	will not

Taking It Further

In formal speech and writing, contractions should be avoided. Rewrite the sentences without contractions.

1 We're going to the party.

We are going to the party.

2 They'd better hurry or we'll all be late.

They had better hurry, or we will all be late.

3 I'd rather go to the movies than rent a video.

I would rather go to the movies than rent a video.

4 I can't stand his bad mood.

I cannot stand his bad mood.

5 They didn't arrive in time, so they couldn't buy the tickets.

They did not arrive in time, so they could not buy the tickets.

6 He'd searched the world for mystery and adventure.

He had searched the world for mystery and adventure.

In the Real World

Find two short advertisements or newspaper headlines that use the apostrophe for contraction and write them in the spaces below.

Example

We've got a huge range of CDs — everything you want!

Answers will vary.

Write the contractions from your examples below. Then, write out the words that form each contraction.

_____

_____

Apostrophes to Show Possession

LESSON 24 PUNCTUATION

The **apostrophe** is also used to show that something belongs to a person or a thing.

Add an apostrophe and an *s* to show possession when a noun is singular.

Example The boy**'s** kite = the kite which belongs to the boy

To show possession when a noun is plural, add only an apostrophe.

Example The girls**'** hats = the hats belonging to the girls

When the plural noun does not end in *-s*, simply add an apostrophe and an *s*.

Example The women**'s** belongings

Try It Out

Rewrite the following sentences to include apostrophes for possession.

1 We have to pass our principals house on the way to school.

    We have to pass our principal's house on the way to school.

2 The dogs kennels were blown over in the storm.

    The dogs' kennels were blown over in the storm.

3 Rosss pen had exploded in the washing machine.

    Ross's pen had exploded in the washing machine.

4 The mens jackets were no longer in the closet.

    The men's jackets were no longer in the closet.

5 The teachers notes were kept in the staff room.

    The teachers'/teacher's notes were kept in the staff room.

6 The childrens bikes were left outside all night.

    The children's bikes were left outside all night.

Taking It Further

Describe where you live and some of the things there. Use the apostrophe for possession where you can.

Example   We live in an apartment. Mom's study is at the front. Next to that is Rick's bedroom . . .

> Answers will vary.

_____

_____

_____

_____

_____

In the Real World

Look at these real-life examples of **incorrect** uses of the apostrophe. Then, rewrite them correctly.

> ## Special today:
> **Banana's**   **Strawberry's**
> **$1**   2 pints for
> per pound   **$2.50**

> ### Clothe's for the whole family:
> **men, women, children and baby's**

> ### Mens dress shirts
> only $9.95 each

bananas, strawberries; clothes, babies; Men's

_____

_____

Periods and Question Marks

LESSON 25
PUNCTUATION

A **period** ends a sentence that makes a statement.

Examples   The teacher was pleased with the whole class.
You can sleep on the bottom bunk.

A **question mark** is used in place of a period to show that the sentence is a question.

Examples   When do you want to go to the mall?
Did he go to the mall?

Try It Out

Complete the sentences by adding the appropriate punctuation: period or question mark.

1   Liz, what are you doing today?_____

2   I think I left my diary at school._____

3   I've got a heap of homework to finish before Friday._____

4   That's my favourite song._____

5   Do you think these colors match?_____

6   May I help you?_____

7   Arthur asked a question without raising his hand._____

8   How about we go out for dinner tonight?_____

Taking It Further

Rewrite the following two paragraphs with periods and question marks. Don't forget to add a capital letter at the beginning of each sentence.

The label said the package contained live sea creature eggs they would hatch within a week of being placed in water I filled a small tank with water and added the contents of the package would the creatures be big enough to see would they look anything like the strange mermaids on the box I couldn't wait to see what happened

The label said the package contained live sea creature eggs. They would hatch

within a week of being placed in water. I filled a small tank with water and

added the contents of the package. Would the creatures be big enough to

see? Would they look anything like the strange mermaids on the box? I couldn't

wait to see what happened.

_____

_____

_____

The princess bent down did she know what she was doing she wasn't sure she
kissed the little toad on his greasy snout the results were sensational the toad
started to grow and change what do you think was there in its place it had
turned into an old man

The princess bent down. Did she know what she was doing? She wasn't sure.

She kissed the little toad on his greasy snout. The results were sensational.

The toad started to grow and change. What do you think was there in its

place? It had turned into an old man.

_____

_____

In the Real World

Calculate and write down the average number of sentences per paragraph in an example of
the following kinds of writing. You can do so by counting periods and question marks in each
example. Then, you can divide that number by the number of paragraphs.

1 a front page newspaper article _____

2 the first page of a book _____

3 a school newsletter or diary _____

4 a business or personal letter _____

Answers will vary.

LESSON 26 Exclamation Points
PUNCTUATION

An **exclamation point** expresses strong feeling and ends a word, group of words, or sentence. The exclamation point should be used sparingly since it is used for dramatic effect.

Examples This is brilliant!
Watch out!

Try It Out

1   Finish the sentences by adding the appropriate punctuation: period or exclamation point. Note that exclamation points are often overused. Think carefully about how you want the sentence to be read before you add one.

| Answers may vary. |

a I just heard some exciting news!_____

b It was too late to stop._____ He wasn't going to make it._____

c You look fantastic!_____

d What a beautiful dress!_____

e Don't worry, everything will be fine._____

f They're the finest athletes the school has ever seen._____

g Don't do it!_____

h "Yes!_____" he shouted. "She's won!_____"

i See you later._____

j It's time to go._____

2   Insert an appropriate period or exclamation point in each space.

First she said she wanted a blue folder, then a green one._ My sister said to try aquamarine._ Then my brother said to go for purple or yellow._ I was impatient and said, "Hurry up and make up your mind already!_"

Taking It Further

1 Write a sentence to express each emotion. Make sure the sentence requires an exclamation mark at the end.

Example   fear _Help! There's a huge spider on my head!_ _____

Sample answers.

a excitement _I can't believe we're almost there!_ _____

b happiness _This is the best sequel yet!_ _____

c frustration _Somebody show me how to open this thing!_ _____

d anger _You and your dog have ruined my new sweater!_ _____

e impatience _Get off the phone so we can leave!_ _____

f amazement _He sure can eat a lot of jalapeños!_ _____

2 Write a six-line skit about a student who surprises a worried parent with good news. When it is completed, read it aloud to a partner.

Student: _Dad, I have to show you something._ _____

Sample answers.

Parent: _It's not your report card, is it?_ _____

Student: _As a matter of fact, it is._ _____

Parent: _Oh boy. Well, let's look at it._ _____

Student: _Here it is._ _____

Parent: _Incredible! This is the best you've ever done!_ _____

In the Real World

Copy four usages of the exclamation point from a book or play that you have read. Check the one that appeals the most to you.

Answers will vary.

1 _____

2 _____

3 _____

4 _____

Commas

LESSON 27
PUNCTUATION

Commas have several functions.

　i Commas are used to separate items in a series.

　　Examples My sister enjoys playing **volleyball, tennis, softball, and basketball.** (series of items)
　　　That was a **silly, predictable, pointless** action movie. (series of three adjectives, each describing the phrase *action movie*)

　ii Commas are used to set off less important information in a sentence.

　　Examples Ms. Kouros, **the new teacher,** is interested in astronomy.
　　　Sean Warne, **who lives in Springfield,** is a great singer.

However, commas should not be used if removing the information would change the meaning of the sentence.

　　Examples My cousin **Dave** is a brilliant computer analyst. (needed to tell which of the cousins)
　　　The person **whom I admire most** is my grandpa. (needed to tell what the speaker is saying about his or her grandpa)

　iii Commas are also used before and after direct speech.

　　Examples "Remember to return your library book today," her mother called.
　　　The guard shouted, "Look out!".

Try It Out

Place commas on either side of the less important information in each sentence.

1　Everyone, whether musical or not, should respect the skill required to play a musical instrument.

2　Melissa, who comes from Canada, is our top student.

3　Smoking, a dangerous habit, is prohibited in public buildings.

4　The elderly man, who was sitting down, looked as if he had had a terrible fright.

5 She looked down, her eyes resting on her ragged shoes, and muttered something that I couldn't hear.

6 In the cave, which is at the far end of the beach, there are some old bones.

Taking It Further

Insert commas where appropriate.

1 Mr. Umble peered into a big, murky, weird bowl full of shimmering, salty water.

2 A small, bright jellyfish at the bottom of the bowl was moving here, there, and everywhere.

3 "I don't think I'll go for a bike ride after all," said Maddy.

4 The teacher finished, "And make sure those assignments are on my desk in the morning."

5 Few people paid much attention to the old train depot, which had stood there for years.

6 "Let me know," Jackie's dad called from the kitchen, "who wins best supporting actor."

7 "I'd like one turkey and cheese, one veggie, and one tuna salad sandwich," requested the hungry boy.

8 Dr. Forester cleaned up the park with the help of his wife, Sandra, and their youngest son, Eric.

In the Real World

Oxydril is a visitor from the planet Absilon in the Outer Galaxy. You are teaching him all about punctuation. In pairs, role-play the lesson in which you teach Oxydril all about commas.

Example   YOU: Oxydril, we put commas in lists of items.
OXYDRIL: Why?
YOU: To keep them apart. Now, we also . . .

Use teaching equipment such as an overhead projector, a whiteboard, or computer technology if such visual aids are appropriate and available.

LESSON 28
PUNCTUATION

Colons and Semicolons

A **colon** is used to introduce lists.

Example Madeleine is known for her fine qualities: compassion, friendliness, humor, modesty, and loyalty.

A colon is also used to introduce explanations, re-statements, or quotations.

Examples There was only one likely result for the hard-working student: academic success.
She ended her speech with a quote from Oscar Wilde: "Maturity is overrated."

Note that in both uses for colons, a complete sentence must precede the colon.

The **semicolon** is used between two closely related sentences that are not joined by a conjunction such as *and* or *but*.

Examples Venus Williams hired a new tennis coach; she thought she needed fresh direction.

Try It Out

Identify the incorrect punctuation in these sentences and correct it by using a colon or semicolon.

Example The good things about the beach are swimming and snorkelling**;** the bad things are sunburn and sand in your lunch.

1 The first spring flowers have appeared**:** tulips, crocus, daffodils.

2 Most people enjoy ice-cream**;** my sister doesn't.

3 He knew the game was up **; or :** he could see them all waiting for him to come out.

4 On my shopping list are many ingredients**:** margarine, milk, bread and cereal.

5 I remember what my granny often said**:** "Be patient, and it will happen."

6 The lawn looks terrible**;** it hasn't rained for ages.

Taking It Further

Write a sentence for each suggestion and use the correct punctuation.

Example   Describe the contents of your book bag. Use a colon.
My bag is crammed with things: books, sports gear, lunch, band music, and goodness knows what else.

1   Write a list of foods you like to eat. Use a colon. | Sample answers. |

Here is a list of my favorite things to eat: burritos, rice, and carrot sticks.

2   Write a piece of advice given to you by a friend or family member. Use a colon.

My mom gave me some good advice: "There's nothing wrong with not knowing

something. Just be willing to ask."

3   Describe a school rule and the reason for it. Use a semicolon.

Students must have a hall pass to leave the room; that way, teachers can

limit the number of people who are not in class.

4   State something that you are proud of. Use a colon to introduce your explanation.

I am proud of my stamp collection: building it took years.

5   Write two contrasting statements. Begin the second with *however* (followed by a comma) and separate the two with a semicolon.

I like to hike in the woods; however, I don't like sleeping in them.

In the Real World

In a book you are currently reading, find one example of the colon and one of the semicolon. Write them below and explain how and why the author used them.

| Answers will vary. |

_____

_____

_____

_____

NAME _____ DATE _____

Quotation Marks in Direct Speech

LESSON 29
PUNCTUATION

> **Direct speech** refers to the words actually spoken by a person. Quotation marks indicate direct speech and are used in pairs.
>
> **Examples** Theo asked Kim, "What time is training?".
> "About 5 p.m.," replied Kim.
> "We are the champions," the supporter sang, "of the world."
>
> Start a new line every time the speaker changes.

Try It Out

Add quotation marks to the sentences.

1 "Where did I put my wrench?" my father called from under the car.

2 Patrick said, "Go two blocks and then look for the bus stop on the right. You can't miss it."

3 "Please turn that music down!" Camille shouted over the noise

4 "I think," said the professor, "that we ought to take a little visit to your cave in the forest."

5 "I think I'd rather clean up the trash than get punished," Shelley whispered to her friend.

6 It seemed like forever, but finally Mom sighed and said, "Oh, I suppose so."

7 "Come on," encouraged her friend. "It's not far from here."

8 "Sharon, would you like to go to a movie with me?" Nick asked.

9 "I really like the energy and skill of the World Cup teams," said Imran.

10 Maya said, "Gas heating is comfortable, but solar heating is the wave of the future."

Taking It Further

Rewrite the following text using appropriate quotation marks to show direct speech. Remember to use a new line for each change of speaker.

> Who is the prettiest of them all? You are, sweetie, for a while, replied the mirror. What do you mean? shouted the queen. That pretty Snow White can't wait to get into this palace, the mirror responded. My foot, she will! cried the queen.

"Who is the prettiest of them all?"

"You are, sweetie, for a while," replied the mirror.

"What do you mean?" shouted the queen.

"That pretty Snow White can't wait to get into this palace," the mirror

responded.

"My foot, she will!" cried the queen.

In the Real World

1   Find out a friend's favorite and least favorite food. Write down your question and the response word for word. Use quotation marks correctly.

Answers will vary.

Question to your friend: _____

_____

Response of your friend: _____

_____

2   Think of your two favorite quotations from movies, songs, friends, parents, or teachers. Write them down in quotation marks and explain in writing why you like them.

_____

_____

_____

_____

LESSON 30 SENTENCES · Declarative Sentences

There are four types of sentences: declarative, interrogative, imperative, and exclamation.

A **declarative sentence** makes a statement that ends with a period.

Examples The national capital, Washington, D.C., is an impressive place to visit.
I love skating and loud music.

Note that like all types of sentences, a declarative sentence must be able to stand on its own as a complete thought.

Try It Out

Put a check next to each complete declarative sentence.

Example Singing loudly in the shower. _____
He was singing loudly in the shower. ✔

1 My dad dropped me off at school today. ✔

2 Tennis, golf and basketball. _____

3 I think I'll go. ✔

4 The dog always yelps with joy when she sees us. ✔

5 Are you ready? _____

6 Considering the time we have left. _____

7 He did it. ✔

8 Walking out the door. _____

Taking It Further

Complete these sentences and punctuate them correctly.

| Sample answers. |

1 The minute I get home, _I take my shoes off._

2 _I learned to play chess_ at my friend's house.

3 As soon as she opened the door, _Marla knew what was wrong._

4 Martin heard _bagpipes playing somewhere down the block._

5 _The talent show ended_ at nine o'clock last night.

6 _A pack of runners dashed_ around the corner and up the street.

7 The baby likes _to sing along with the radio._

8 _Desmond grabbed his backpack_ and walked out the door.

In the Real World

The introductory paragraph of a newspaper article will usually contain one or more declarative sentences.

Example

Thrill of victory, agony of the feet

A local sixth-grader has won the annual National Rotten Sneaker Contest. Proudly holding his trophy, Mark Hampton explained the secret to his success.

Make up the next two paragraphs that summarize the event and its conclusion. Make sure you use complete sentences.

Answers will vary.

_____

_____

_____

_____

_____

_____

_____

_____

_____

_____

 **Imperative Sentences**

An **imperative sentence** gives a command or makes a request. Imperative sentences often begin with a verb and end with a period or an exclamation point. In the examples below, the understood subject is the pronoun *you.*

Examples **Read** silently to concentrate on the story.
              Leave the room immediately!

Note that like all types of sentences, an imperative sentence must be able to stand on its own as a complete thought.

Try It Out

Underline the imperative sentences in the following passage. Then, write a paragraph about Gretel tricking the wicked witch. Include three imperative sentences.

"Climb into the oven. See if it's hot enough," said the witch.

"How am I supposed to do that?" Gretel asked, realizing what the witch had in store for her. "Please show me how."

Answers will vary.

_____

_____

_____

_____

_____

_____

_____

Taking It Further

Change the following declarative sentences into imperative sentences. Number each instruction.

First, you put the key into the lock of the car door and turn it. Then, you open the car door. Next, you sit in the driver's seat. You then should use the little key to unlock the bar on the steering wheel. You take the bar off the steering wheel. Finally, you can use the car key to start the ignition.

1 Put the key into the lock of the car door and turn it.

2 Open the car door.

3 Sit in the driver's seat.

4 Use the little key to unlock the bar on the steering wheel.

5 Take the bar off the steering wheel.

6 Use the car key to turn on the ignition.

In the Real World

List four commands that your parents would *never* say to you!

Example   Play ear-splitting music.
Don't do your homework.

Answers will vary.

Now list four commands that your teacher would *never* say to you.

Answers will vary.

LESSON 32 SENTENCES **Joining Sentences with Conjunctions**

You can use **conjunctions** to join two or more shorter sentences. Combining sentences helps you connect ideas and add variety to your writing.

Example I went out to lunch with Toby. I like him a lot.
I went out to lunch with Toby **because** I like him a lot.

Try It Out

Join each of the following pairs of sentences with the conjunction provided to make one sentence.

Example The cat was a friendly tabby. It purred when I cuddled it. (which)

➜ The cat, which was a friendly tabby, purred when I cuddled it.

Answers may vary.

1 Dorothy was a smart person. She won the district spelling bee three times. (who)

Dorothy, who was a smart person, won the district spelling bee three times.

2 The Pacific Ocean is the largest in the world. It has more than 20,000 islands. (and)

The Pacific Ocean is the largest in the world and has more than 20,000

islands.

3 The cyclists were riding along the path. They suddenly braked for an armadillo. (when)

The cyclists were riding along the path when they suddenly braked for

an armadillo.

4 It was raining. The couple caught the train. (so)

It was raining, so the couple caught the train.

5 Donna was frustrated. She couldn't understand what the problem was. (because)

Donna was frustrated because she couldn't understand what the

problem was.

6 Sharif was tired. He went to swimming practice at 6 a.m. (although)

Although Sharif was tired, he went to swimming practice at 6 a.m.

_____

7 How can I finish my homework? You expect me to do my chores every night. (when)

How can I finish my homework when you expect me to do my chores

every night?

8 Tim isn't able to help. He isn't willing, either. (neither, nor)

Tim is neither able nor willing to help.

Taking It Further

Recall five activities you did today. Write each in a short sentence below. Then, use conjunctions to write the same information in three or fewer sentences.

Answers will vary.

_____

_____

_____

In the Real World

Write a special request for a birthday present by joining sentences with conjunctions.

Answers will vary.

_____

_____

LESSON 33 Subjects and Verbs
SENTENCES

Most sentences make statements. The two most important elements of a sentence are the **subject** and the **verb**.

subject   verb

Example The **dog chased** the cat.

An easy way to identify the subject is to ask "Who?" or "What?" before the verb.

Example Nayan hit the ball out of the stadium.
Question: Who hit the ball? Answer: Nayan.
Nayan is the subject of the sentence.

Remember: The subject and verb should agree in number and person.

Person	Number	
	Singular	**Plural**
1st	I	we
2nd	you	you
3rd	he/she/it	they

Try It Out

1 For each of the following sentences, circle the verb that agrees with the subject.

a Whenever Sam (play / plays) soccer, he comes home covered in mud.

b We (is / are) very happy with the result.

c Elite athletes (trains / train) extremely hard in their chosen sports.

d Trucks (carries / carry) some very heavy loads.

e There (was / were) hundreds of people at the performance.

f Everybody (is / are) allowed to go on the field trip.

2 Complete the following sentences by adding a verb and other words to each subject.

Example   The firefighter **doused the flames**.

a The pigeon _looked at me hungrily._

b Martians _have never been discovered._

c Trees _line the road into the park._

d You _will certainly like this next song._

e My sister _is almost as tall as Dad._

f We _meet at the monument every Saturday._

Taking It Further

Construct a sentence using each verb in parentheses. Then, underline the subject in each sentence.

1 (swerved) _The taxi swerved left at the last minute._

2 (denies) _Lara denies leaving the refrigerator open._

3 (have known) _You have known Mr. Lozano the longest._

4 (lost) _According to Ben, he lost his wallet around here._

5 (will play) _Meiying will play clarinet in the school band._

6 (seem) _Whatever you say, you seem upset._

7 (goes) _A ferry goes across the bay five times a day._

8 (is leaving) _Next year Ms. Galler is leaving to work somewhere else._

In the Real World

Write a sentence on each of the subjects below, making sure that the subject agrees with the verb.

> A pack of really ugly animals
> The most gorgeous person in the universe
> Yourself

Example   These hyenas were so ugly that their looks could curdle milk.

Sentence Fragments

A **sentence fragment** is a set of words that is punctuated to look like a sentence but is not complete.

Example The race. My destiny.

These groups of words are not sentences because they lack verbs. Add a verb to create one sentence: The race was my destiny.

Some professional writers use sentence fragments for dramatic effect. Doing so can be appropriate in play scripts, poetry, and fiction.

In most writing, however, you should avoid sentence fragments because they can be confusing and appear to result from carelessness.

Try It Out

Rewrite each sentence fragment or set of fragments as a complete sentence.

Example   The buzzer. Victory.
                The buzzer signaled our victory.

Answers may vary.

1 Outside! Right now.

   Get/Go outside right now.

2 The rainbow. Beautiful.

   The rainbow is so beautiful.

3 A fantastic night!

   That was a fantastic night!

4 In through the back door, up the stairs, and straight to bed.

   She went in through the back door, up the stairs, and straight to bed.

5 Something glistening in the dark.

   I thought I saw something glistening in the dark.

6 From far away, the sad call of a bugle.

   From far away we heard the sad call of a bugle.

Taking It Further

As mentioned, there are times when a fragment can be used for dramatic effect. Choose one scenario below, and write a paragraph on it. Try to create suspense or excitement by using at least one sentence fragment. Underline any sentence fragments you use.

Example   "Shh! Stop talking. I thought I heard something. <u>Footsteps? No,</u> <u>perhaps a voice.</u> What do you think? Oh, no, it's Mr. Beamish!"

"Oh, hello, Mr. Beamish!" said Martin nervously.

"What do you think you're doing here?"

1   A rock climber is about to reach the top of a cliff when she feels her rope slip.

2   You are at an inter-school athletics competition. Your school is doing very well. Your best friend is at the starting line for the next race and if he or she wins, your school will win the championship.

3   A holiday fireworks display ends with an amazing finale, full of many different sights and sounds.

Answers will vary.

_____

_____

_____

_____

_____

In the Real World

Find three examples of sentence fragments in a story or another piece of writing, and rewrite them as complete sentences below. Discuss with a partner what you think the writer is trying to achieve with these sentence fragments.

Answers will vary.

_____

_____

_____

LESSON 35 Stringy Sentences

SENTENCES

A sentence should focus on one main idea. Writers sometimes tack on one idea after another. The result is a **stringy sentence** that is awkward and difficult to read.

Stringy   I struggled to keep afloat, and the lifesaver eventually reached me far out from shore, and I was thankful for my rescue.

Revised   I struggled to keep afloat. The lifesaver eventually reached me far out from shore. I was thankful for my rescue.

To correct stringy sentences, decide how many shorter sentences you want to create. Remember to start each sentence with a capital letter.

Try It Out

Correct the stringy sentences below by rewriting them as shorter sentences.

1   At the circus, we saw the clowns and trapeze artists, and I especially liked the tightrope-walker.

At the circus, we saw the clowns and trapeze artists. | Answers may vary. |

I especially liked the tightrope-walker.

2   We had a great time at Luna Park and really enjoyed the rides, but I got tired after walking around for a few hours and wanted to go home, but the others hadn't spent all their money yet.

We had a great time at Luna Park and really enjoyed the rides.

I got tired after walking around for a few hours, though. I wanted to go home,

but the others hadn't spent all their money yet.

3 First, he went to the skateboard park to see if Tom was there, and then he decided to try the local shopping mall, but he had no luck, and in the end he thought he might as well go home and wait for Tom to turn up when he was ready.

First, he went to the skateboard park to see if Tom was there. Then, he

decided to try the local shopping mall. He had no luck. In the end he thought

he might as well go home and wait for Tom to turn up when he was ready.

_____

Taking It Further

Write a stringy sentence passage on the lines provided, and then swap it with a partner. Rewrite your partner's sentence in shorter sentences.

| Answers will vary. |

_____

_____

_____

In the Real World

Poets often use language creatively. They may write in sentence fragments or run thoughts together in stringy sentences.

The following poem has no punctuation and has several ideas that are strung along, one after another. Rewrite it with proper punctuation and in shorter sentences. Discuss the difference between your version and the original. Which do you like better and why?

    you and the cool kids
    kept me at arm's length
    and played your games without me
    so that I wouldn't tell on you
    or so you thought
    but it's not easy when the principal is Mom

You and the cool kids kept me at arm's length.

| Answers may vary. |

You played your games without me so that I wouldn't tell on you—or so you

thought. It's not easy when the principal is Mom.

LESSON 36 Phrases

SENTENCES

A **phrase** is a group of words within a sentence. It cannot stand alone, but it provides extra information.

Example **After the rain**, the girls played. (The phrase *after the rain* tells you when the girls played.)

A phrase often starts with a preposition, such as *after, above, at, without, of, under, since,* or *between* (see Lesson 19).

Example **Since** the old days, my family has farmed.

A phrase can start with a participle (see Lesson 12).

Example **Watching** carefully, she knew every move.
Caught on video, the player had no excuse.

A phrase can appear anywhere in a sentence.

Example One **of numerous casualties,** my grandfather luckily survived the war **despite the horrendous death toll.**

Try It Out

Underline the phrase(s) in each sentence below.

1 After one last look around, Paddy closed the door.

2 There on the sofa she lay between a pile of laundry and her faithful dog.

3 Steph stood at the top of the hill.

4 Hearing my name called, I snapped awake.

5 At the stroke of one, the mouse ran down the clock.

6 My brother's shirt, stained permanently, was a lost cause.

7 The bus stalled in the middle of the highway, stranding its passengers.

8 Abandoned by its mother, the kitten looked weak and dejected.

Taking It Further

1 Add one or more phrases to each of the following sentences.

a He strolled _along the lake in deep thought._

b Zoe grabbed the rope _hanging from the tree branch._

c The little boy jumped _off the high dive_

d _Gripping the baking pan firmly_ _____, I put the cake in the oven.

e _Under cover of darkness_ _____, they made their plan.

f _Deeply moved by the beautiful scenery_ _____, she drew a picture.

2 Write two sentences that include phrases beginning with participles. Underline the phrases.

Example   Caught in the glare of the headlights, the cat froze.

a _____

b _____

3 Write two sentences that include phrases beginning with prepositions. Place the phrases in different parts of the sentences, and underline the phrases.

Example   On top of the world after his test, he did a dance.

a _____

b _____

In the Real World

Newspaper headlines often use phrases rather than complete sentences. Write a headline phrase for each of the following: sports, entertainment, and current events.

Example   (entertainment) Critics Divided on Film

_____

_____

_____

 **Clauses**

SENTENCES

A **clause** is a group of words that contains a subject and a verb. There are two types of clauses: **main clauses** and **subordinate clauses**.

   i A **main clause** usually makes complete sense on its own and expresses the basic meaning of the sentence.

     Example The skiers raced in twilight.

A sentence can have more than one main clause.

          main clause   main clause

     Example The party stopped, and the guests complained.

   ii A **subordinate clause** is less important than the main clause. It offers extra information about the main clause and cannot stand alone. Subordinate clauses often begin with a conjunction such as *if, that, when,* or *because.*

          main clause   subordinate clause

     Example The skiers raced in twilight **because they were risk-takers**.

Try It Out

Underline the main clause(s) and put parentheses around the subordinate clauses in each sentence below.

   Example (Although my dog is timid), my cat is aggressive.

1 (Because the exam was difficult,) the teacher gave a practice test.

2 The batter set a home run record (while the fans cheered.)

3 The spaceship took off slowly and then suddenly vanished.

4 This is the house (where my dad was born.)

5 (Unless people give to charity,) poor families will suffer.

6 Jenny was sure (that Sarah was planning a surprise party for her.)

7 I decided to take a taxi home (since it was getting late.)

8 I like bananas, but my sister prefers oranges.

Taking It Further

Complete the following sentences with an appropriate main or subordinate clause. Identify which type of clause you add, M = main, S = subordinate.

Example   We left the concert **as soon as the music finished. (S)**

1   I love my parents because _____   Answers will vary.   S

2   I liked fifth grade, although _____   S

3   When she heard about the theft of all the costumes, _____   M

4   If you want to play something else, _____   M

5   My family is fun when _____   S

6   After the bad weather, _____   M

7   Rick could surf all day where _____   S

8   Unless you say it slowly, _____   M

In the Real World

Write a few lines on an issue about which you feel strongly. Use main and subordinate clauses appropriately. You may choose one of the following topics or your own subject: after-school detentions, bullying, the environment.

Example   Looking after our environment is very important because it affects many parts of our lives. If the air or water is polluted, our health can suffer. We must pull together and help clean up our planet.

Answers will vary.

_____

_____

_____

_____

 **LESSON 38** SENTENCES **Paragraphs (1)**

A **paragraph** is made up of several sentences. A paragraph usually begins with a **topic sentence** that states the main idea. All the other sentences in the paragraph are related to the topic sentence.

Example

Maria is a generous girl. She volunteered to raise money for the United Way Appeal at her school. Nobody knew she also donated her savings. Maria is motivated by concern for others.

- The idea introduced in the topic sentence is developed in the rest of the paragraph.
- Supporting sentences should be relevant and presented in a logical order.
- A well-written paragraph connects clearly to other paragraphs.

Try It Out

Read these run-on paragraphs carefully and indicate where they need to be divided into two paragraphs.

Love or hate them, sports are very popular in the United States. Millions of Americans compete in a huge variety of sports, from football to gymnastics. Others prefer just to be spectators so that they can cheer on participants from the stands or their couches. People often develop their love of sports ¶ in childhood. Watching particular sports with parents and other family members sets a strong example. Playing little league baseball or soccer can also spark an interest.

Taking It Further

1   Write a topic sentence for each subject.

Example   pets: <u>Pets are popular companions for kids and adults.</u>

a a sport

<u>Many people enjoy basketball for its action</u>

<u>and team play.</u>

Sample answers.

b cars

Rising gas prices have increased sales of cars that get better mileage.

c a holiday

Sometime in mid-December, I start thinking about my New Year's

resolutions.

d friends

While most of us know quite a few people, true friends are rare.

2 Write a paragraph based on one of your topic sentences from above. You will need to add
interesting details to support the topic sentence.

Answers will vary.

In the Real World

Write a first paragraph for this headline. Think carefully about your topic sentence.

Reunited After Fifty Years

Answers will vary.

LESSON 39 SENTENCES

Paragraphs (2)

This lesson builds on Lesson 38, in which you learned that a paragraph usually begins with a **topic sentence** that states a main idea. The other sentences in the paragraph give two or three supporting points.

In the next few years, you will be expected to express your opinions in essays. You can practice for these essays by writing three paragraphs, each with a topic sentence and two or three supporting points.

Below is a report on energy resources. Read it and note the topic and supporting sentences in each paragraph.

Paragraph 1

Topic sentence → The energy you use every time you turn on a light or ride in a car has to come

pporting sentences
1
2
3

from somewhere. In recent years, people have paid more attention to where that energy comes from. For over a century, we have relied largely on non-renewable resources, substances that will eventually run out. Renewable resources, on the other hand, can be replaced.

Paragraph 2

Topic sentence → Nonrenewable resources include such important fuels as oil and natural gas.

pporting sentences
1
2

These substances power our cars, trucks, and trains and generate much of our electricity. Supplies of such resources are limited, however, and will eventually decrease over time.

Paragraph 3

Topic sentence → Renewable resources promise unlimited energy, but that goal is far off.

pporting sentences
1
2
3

Electricity can be generated from wind or sunlight. Fuel cells offer a renewable source of energy to power cars without pollution. All of these resources need more development, however, before they become common and affordable.

Try It Out

Read the following three paragraphs written by a student on the question "Why is it important to develop renewable sources of energy?". Write down the topic sentence, and bullet-point the supporting ideas for each paragraph.

Even though I can't drive, I see my parents spending more and more on gas and complaining about our electric bill. One of the reasons these costs increase is that supplies of energy are limited. The more people need fuel, the more expensive it is.

A major problem with nonrenewable fuels is that they generate pollution. Burning gasoline and coal dirties the air. In some places, air pollution causes serious health problems as a result.

Many renewable resources like solar and wind power do not pollute. The only problem is that they're expensive to develop. Making them a major source of energy would require a lot more work. If we put as much "energy" into renewable resources as we do into oil, maybe that dream would become a reality.

Topic sentence 1: _Even though I can't drive, I see my parents spending more and more on gas and complaining about our electric bill._

- _Energy supplies are limited._
- _Price depends on how many people need fuel._

Topic sentence 2: _A major problem with nonrenewable fuels is that they generate pollution._

- _Gasoline and coal pollute._
- _Air pollution causes health problems._

Topic sentence 3: _Many renewable resources like solar and wind power do not pollute._

- _Developing them requires money and work, though._
- _Increased effort could make renewable energy available._

Taking It Further

Now it is your turn to write three paragraphs about young people participating in efforts to use energy more responsibly.

1 Write two or three supporting ideas in brief sentences below each topic sentence.

Topic sentence 1 Even students can take steps to save nonrenewable energy sources and promote renewable resources.

Answers will vary.

- _____

- _____

- _____

Topic sentence 2 Saving gas and electricity is not difficult but may require changing our usual habits.

- _____

- _____

- _____

Topic sentence 3 Getting involved in efforts to use and increase renewable resources is not limited to adults.

- _____

- _____

- _____

2 In pairs, read another student's bullet points. Discuss any differences or difficulties in working out the points. Then, if necessary, add any appropriate changes to your own bullet points above.

In the Real World

Use the above outline to write three paragraphs below. If you prefer to state and support your own opinions about energy resources, feel free to do so.

Answers will vary.

_____

_____

_____

_____

_____

_____

NAME _____ DATE _____

Vocabulary

Some of the most common errors in spelling come from words that sound alike but are different in spelling and meaning. These words are called **homophones**.

Examples sum, some   their, there, they're   than, then   its, it's   bear, bare

To help learn the correct spelling, it helps if you can identify and understand the part that each word plays in a sentence. In other words, understanding how a word is used can help you improve your spelling.

Try It Out

1   Solve the following word search puzzle by circling five pairs of homophones. Write each pair on the lines provided.

L	S	F	T	I	L	T	L	T	I	O
S	E	L	L	J	I	E	E	H	C	L
M	T	E	O	A	A	O	S	E	W	E
E	W	A	I	S	T	A	H	F	A	W
I	H	W	V	T	E	S	T	L	S	C
M	O	L	G	U	E	I	G	H	T	E
F	L	E	E	W	T	H	O	L	E	L
D	E	N	L	W	Y	E	I	A	H	L

ate/eight, cell/sell, flea/flee, hole/whole, waist/waste

_____

_____

2   Now choose the appropriate words from above to complete the following sentences.

   a For Thanksgiving, we basically ____*ate*____ food and watched football.

   b Under the microscope, the ____*cell*____ looked like an inner tube.

   c Everyone managed to ____*flee*____ the burning building in time.

d The dog ate the _____whole_____ leg of lamb, so we missed our main course!

e Recycling encourages us not to _____waste_____ plastic and paper by throwing them out. Instead, they can be used again.

Taking It Further

Write a sentence that shows the correct usage and spelling of any three sets of the following homophones.

bear, bare	here, hear	sum, some	their, they're there	to, too, two

Answers will vary.

1 _____

_____

2 _____

_____

3 _____

_____

_____

In the Real World

Write down as many homophone pairs (or triples) as you can in five minutes. Then, see how many you can squeeze into a single sentence. See Lessons 43 and 44 if you need help.

Example   "They're over there in their lair," said the bare bear, "combing their hair when they should be chasing the hare."

Answers will vary.

_____

_____

_____

_____

 **LESSON 41** **VOCABULARY** # Using a Spell-Checker

Today we have the benefit of a computer spell-checker to correct errors in our writing. However, we must not leave all the thinking to the computer. The computer cannot spot words that are spelled right but used incorrectly, such as writing *your* instead of *you're*.

Take time to learn common spelling mistakes, especially those that involve homophones. Remember, these are words that sound the same but have a different spelling and meaning (see Lesson 40).

The following sets of words are homophones:

- tail, tale
- son, sun
- their, they're, there
- aloud, allowed
- wait, weight
- where, wear

Try It Out

1 Find homophones for each of the following words.

> **Example**   rain: **rein, reign**

   a stair _stare_   **d** red _read_

   b no _know_   **e** sew _so, sow_

   c one _won_   **f** bye _by, buy_

2 A computer spell-checker often misses errors in usage. You must identify such errors yourself. For each sentence below, circle the correct word in parentheses.

   a (It's / its) Jessica's birthday tomorrow.

   b (Their / There / They're) goes that cool sports car again.

   c Can you show me (your / you're) notes for a minute?

   d If (your / you're) lucky, I'll save you a piece of chicken.

   e That old sign has lost most of (its / it's) paint.

f Brad and Janie told me to meet at (they're /(their)/ there) house after school.

g My parents are away. (There / Their /(They're)) visiting my aunt.

h That dog is dangerous, and (it's /(its)) temper is unpredictable.

Taking It Further

Rewrite this passage with correct spelling. (Note that a spell-checker would identify only three of the following nine errors.)

> When Dave asked wear I wanted to goe on vacation, I new the anser right away.
>
> "The beech, of coarse," I said. "But can we avoid peek season? Their are allways so many people then."

When Dave asked where I wanted to go on vacation, I knew the answer

right away.

"The beach, of course," I said. "But can we avoid peak season? There are

always so many people then."

In the Real World

Make a list of your six most common spelling errors below. Then, write a very short story (no more than 200 words), spelling all six words correctly. Underline the six words and try to memorize the correct spelling of each.

Answers will vary.

LESSON 42 VOCABULARY: Using a Dictionary

A **dictionary** is a book that lists words in alphabetical order with their meanings. Many dictionaries also provide a word's pronunciation, part of speech, and history.

Example Inspirational people show us **fortitude**.
fortitude (**for**-tih-tood) *noun:* patient courage or strength.

Try It Out

Follow the prompts to work out the meanings of the following words. | Answers will vary. |

1 "Carla was *chagrined* by the discovery that her hard work had been wasted."

Write down what you think *chagrined* means. _____

Are you sure you know its meaning? Read the dictionary definition and check if your answer is correct.

> **chagrined** (shuh-**grihnd**) [from French *chagrin,* sad] *adjective:* embarrassed or disappointed by failure: "The chagrined losers refused to shake hands after the game."

2 "Reading more has had a positive *affect/effect* on my writing."

a Circle what you think is the correct usage of the word in italics above.

Are you sure you know the difference between the commonly mistaken words *affect* (verb) and *effect* (noun)?

b Read the dictionary definition below. Each numbered example gives you a context for the appropriate meaning.

> **effect** (ih-**fekt**) *noun:* 1. result: "Grandma's cancer is an effect of smoking." 2. power to influence someone or something: "Road construction has had a negative effect on business in the area." 3. an intended appearance: "Wanda likes to wear strange clothes for effect."

c Check if your answer above is correct.

d Now look up the dictionary definition of *affect*, and write it below. Make up your own sentence to show the meaning of the verb.

Answers will vary.

_____

_____

Taking It Further

Write down what you think are the meanings of the following words. Then, use the dictionary to check your answers.

Answers may vary.

1 formidable _causing fear or amazement_____

2 personnel _group of people available to do work_____

3 wrath _fierce anger_____

4 replenish _to fill or restore_____

5 infamous _having a bad reputation_____

6 clandestine _secret_____

7 medicinal _used to cure sickness_____

8 liberty _the condition of being free from outside control___

In the Real World

Create a page with the heading "My New Words." As you read for class, write in the words you do not know. Use the dictionary to expand your knowledge of the world and the English language.

My new words	
New Word	**Definition**

LESSON 43 Tricky Spelling
VOCABULARY

Here are some important rules that can help improve your spelling.

i When the sound is "ee," put *i* before *e* except after *c*.

Examples thief, piece, yield, ceiling, deceive, receipt

Note: Some words do not follow this rule: *either, neither, seize, weird,* and so on.

ii To form the plural of a word ending in *y*, change the *y* to *i* and add *es*.

Examples fly, flies; spy, spies; country, countries; study, studies

iii The rule above applies to words that have a consonant before the *y*. If there is a vowel before the *y*, form the plural by adding *s*.

Examples essay, essays; donkey, donkeys; journey, journeys

Try It Out

Write a sentence using each of these easily confused words correctly.

Example   accept / except

I accept your apology.

Ron works late every day except Friday.

1 principal / principle

Our principal will visit class today.

Sample answers.

These rules are based on the principle of respect.

2 of / off

Solitaire is one of my favorite card games.

Thawing icicles started to fall off the gutters.

3 stationary / stationery

The frightened deer stood completely stationary.

Brenda still writes letters by hand on her own stationery.

4 weather / whether

Have you heard the weather forecast for today?

I don't know whether we'll make it on time.

5 capital / capitol

Salt Lake City is the capital of Utah.

State business is conducted in the capitol building.

Taking It Further

1 Check the spelling of the following words. Put a check by those that are correct, and rewrite those that are incorrect.

cheif _chief_   recieve _receive_

deceit ✔   wierd _weird_

2 Change the following words into plurals.

army _armies_   monkey _monkeys_

lady _ladies_   holiday _holidays_

In the Real World

Look in some magazines or newspapers, and find some misspellings or errors that make for funny reading. Alternatively, have fun writing down the wrong word (called a malapropism) in a sentence.

Examples   Much of the government's work is done by civil serpents.
(should be *civil servants*)

The flood damage was so bad that they had to evaporate the city.
(should be *evacuate*)

Answers will vary.

_____

_____

_____

LESSON 44 VOCABULARY · Tips for Spelling Correctly

Words with tricky spellings have to be learned. Here is one method for learning them, using the word *absence* as an example.

1 Copy the word and say it aloud to yourself. Then, split the word into its sound units (syllables): ab/sence.

2 Write a brief memory prompt by focusing on a letter or letters that cause the confusion. The second part of the word ends in *ce*, not *se* (as in *sense*). Your memory prompt might be "The *sence* in *absence* ends in *ce*."

3 Learn a small number of spelling words (four to six) this way each night, and then ask a member of your family or another student to test you.

Remember that finding a way to learn a word will help your brain remember the tricky spelling.

Commonly Misspelled Words

absence	burglar	education	independence	neither
accident	business	embarrass	innocent	nuisance
accurate	busy	exaggerate	interrupt	
achieve		existence		occasionally
architect	cannot	extraordinary	jealous	occur
address	character			occurrence
adolescent	chief	forty	laboratory	often
already	choose	friend	library	opportunity
always	coarse	foreign	lieutenant	opposite
anniversary	committee		likeable	
anonymous	conscience	grammar	literature	parallel
answer	conscious	grief	loose (adj.)	peculiar
	courage	guarantee	lose (v.)	picnic
beautiful	course			piece
believe	criticism	hear	manageable	pleasant
benefit		here	marriage	pleasure
bicycle	deceive	heaven	millennium	politics
biscuit	delicious	height	minimum	precede
brake	difference	hole	minute	presence
break	disappointed		mischievous	presents
breakfast	dissatisfied	ignorance		proceed
breath (n.)	does	immature	negligence	
breathe (v.)		immediately	neighbor	

quiet	separate	through	vegetable	wholly
quite	sincere	too	vehicle	woman
	sincerely	to	waist	women
recent		two	waste	writing
resent	taught	truly	weather	write
recommend	taut		whether	wrote
reign	their	unconscious	where	written
rain	there	unusual	which	
rhythm	thorough	useable	witch	your
ridiculous	though	usually	whole	you're

Confusing Words

Some words might sound similar but have different meanings and uses. It helps to know the word's part of speech as well as its dictionary meaning.

Read the list below, and check at least three word groups that you find confusing or did not know. Then, write a sentence for each word showing its proper use in a sentence.

accept (v. to receive)
except (prep. not including)

advice (n. recommendation)
advise (v. to give advice)

affect (v. to influence)
effect (n. result or impact)

confidant (n. someone you tell secrets to)
confident (adj. sure, certain)

persecute (v. to harass)
prosecute (v. to start legal action)

cite (v. refer to)
sight (n. sense of vision)
site (n. place, location)

Answers will vary.

_____

_____

_____

_____

_____

_____

_____

Three Spelling Tests

Circle the correct spelling in each of the pairs below. Then, cover the word and write it correctly from memory. Finally, check to see if you spelled it correctly.

Test 1

1 lonly / (lonely)   lonely _____
2 (separate) / seperate   separate _____
3 (receive) / recieve   receive _____
4 truely / (truly)   truly _____
5 grammer / (grammar)   grammar _____
6 existance / (existence)   existence _____
7 (rhythm) / rithym   rhythm _____
8 independant / (independent)   independent _____
9 (embarrass) / embarass   embarrass _____
10 usable / (useable)   useable _____

Test 2

1 succede / (succeed)   succeed _____
2 priviledge / (privilege) privilege _____
3 (extraordinary) / extrordinary   extraordinary _____
4 picnick / (picnic)   picnic _____
5 (absence) / absense   absence _____
6 repitition / (repetition) repetition _____
7 (relevant) / relevent   relevant _____
8 (mischievous) / mischievious   mischievous _____
9 parallell / (parallel)   parallel _____
10 allready / (already)   already _____

Test 3

Now it's your turn to write a spelling test, like the first two tests, for your partner in class. Ask your partner to identify some troublesome spelling words from the list of commonly misspelled words. Choose ten words from the list, and create a misspelling for each. Write the pairs below, and have your partner choose the correct spelling in each pair. After you check your partner's answers, don't forget to swap roles so your partner gives you a spelling test. Have fun and improve your spelling!

Partner's name: _____

> Answers will vary.

1 _____

2 _____

3 _____

4 _____

5 _____

6 _____

7 _____

8 _____

9 _____

10 _____

Reminder: Record the corrections to any misspelled words in your notebook. Learn spelling as an important part of your homework and self-development.

LESSON (45) **Writing in Context**

A Brief Narrative and a Personal Letter

Read the following **narrative** (a story with a sequence of events). As you do, think about how the writer has followed the boxed guidelines to create a good example of descriptive, action-based writing.

A Childhood or Recent Incident

(1) One Sunday afternoon when I was about nine years old, I remember sitting near the toddlers' pool at our community center. It was an uncomfortable day, the air still and hot. I sat under a big tree with drooping branches, but its shade didn't help much. Suddenly, my brother, who was dipping his feet in the water,

(2) shouted, "This is boring! Let's go to the big-boy pool." Before I had a chance to reply, he quickly bolted over the green grass toward the Olympic-sized pool.   (3)

(4) I followed him because I had nothing better to do. He was so fast, running like a bull charging down a busy street, that I could barely hear him yell, "C'mon!". Then something incredible happened, and all I could do was watch in shock.

He spun around in mid air—a full 360-degree turn—and then landed flat on his   (5) back, right on the soggy green grass. He had run top speed into a stringy white rope that was supposed to keep people off the wet lawn! He hadn't seen it; lucky for him, he was only shaken up. I never ran after my brother again after that.

---

(1) Specify the place and describe location. Indicate time and place. Give the reader a good picture of the scene.

(2) Use dialogue to add personal appeal.

(3) Use specific action words. For example, the verb *bolted* helps the reader "see" how the brother ran. It also builds suspense: What's going to happen in the next paragraph?

(4) Use comparisons and adjectives that appeal to the senses.

(5) Build to a climactic moment of action with a brief mention of the outcome.

Now it is your turn to practice your story-writing skills. Write three paragraphs about a specific event, either from childhood or a recent incident (maximum total words: 200). The story can be true or fictional.

- Plan your story details. Where will it occur? Who will the characters be? What problem will they face and how will they solve it?

- As you write, use action verbs to show what happened. Also, use specific nouns and adjectives to help the reader picture your story.

A Childhood or Recent Incident

Answers will vary.

_____

_____

_____

_____

_____

_____

_____

_____

_____

_____

_____

_____

_____

_____

_____

_____

Trade stories with a partner and evaluate his or her writing using this sheet.

ASSESSMENT SHEET: Brief Narrative

Student Name: _____

Teacher: _____

Date: _____

Task: Write a brief story of an event, real or imagined.

Length: Write three well-developed paragraphs.

Criteria	Very High	High	Medium	Medium-Low	Low
1 Described the event with a clear three-paragraph sequence; characters were lively and believable	5	4	3	2	1
2 Established a clear sense of time and place	5	4	3	2	1
3 Used appropriate and expressive language, particularly action verbs, vivid adjectives, and brief dialogue	5	4	3	2	1
4 Followed conventions for correct spelling, punctuation, sentence structure, and paragraphing	5	4	3	2	1

Total score: /20

Overall Level: Very High / High / Medium / Medium-Low / Low (Circle)

Comments:

_____

_____

_____

_____

_____

_____

How to Write a Personal Letter on an Issue

A **personal letter** tells another person something about your opinions and beliefs, even your troubles and fears. It's a way of describing your feelings and looking forward to a considerate response.

Many authors of popular adolescent novels and stories receive and reply to letters from readers. Writing an author gives you the opportunity to discuss an issue that arises from discussions or thoughts about your reading. Read the following letter written, but not mailed, by a reader of Lockie Leonard's adventures.

77 Mockingbird Drive
Lenexa, KS 66215

① Address

② Capital letters for proper nouns

September 20, 2005

③ Leave a line between the address and date.

Dear Mr. Winton:

I really enjoyed reading your novel about Lockie Leonard and I wanted to ask you more about family life. ④

In our class, we talked about fathers, and I thought that having a cop for a dad, like Lockie, would be pretty funny. He might give me a ticket for turning up late for breakfast! I have trouble getting up with the alarm, and I wanted to know if some dads lose their sense of humor when they get caught up with work and have so many things to do. ⑤

My dad works late at the office. I think it would be really cool if we could go to the lake together. Lockie's got the right idea about how to have fun. How do you think I can get Dad to come around to the idea without him talking about my homework? ⑥

Please write soon. I can't wait to read the next book about Lockie. ⑦

Yours sincerely,

Tina Staples ⑧ Sign your name and print your full name beneath the signature.

④ **Introduction:** Begin with an enthusiastic or friendly comment, and briefly state your specific interest or concern.

⑤ **Paragraph 2:** Give detailed information on the issue you are writing to discuss. Connect your life to an incident in the story. Balance facts with humor or other informal but appropriate language.

⑥ **Paragraph 3:** Specify your request or concern so that the reader knows the point of your letter. A question helps to focus your reader's response.

⑦ **Paragraph 4:** End with a brief and sincere note of appreciation and expectation of a reply.

Now it is your turn to write a letter of three paragraphs to an author or friend. Choose an issue that arises from something you have read.

- First, jot down your thoughts and talk about the issue with a classmate or your teacher. What issue are you writing about? Why? What is your position on the issue?

- As you write, state your issue and fully explain your reasons for your position. Refer to at least one specific event, and limit your response to 200 words.

Answers will vary.

_____

_____

_____

_____

_____

_____

_____

_____

_____

_____

_____

Trade letters with a partner and evaluate his or her writing using this sheet.

ASSESSMENT SHEET: Personal Letter

Student Name: _____

Teacher: _____

Date: _____

Task: Write a brief personal letter, based on an issue raised in a reading.

Length: Three paragraphs and no more than 200 words total

Criteria	Very High	High	Medium	Medium-Low	Low
1 Stated the issue and clearly explained reasons in support; wrote three well-developed paragraphs	5	4	3	2	1
2 Established a friendly and considerate tone	5	4	3	2	1
3 Used appropriate and expressive language	5	4	3	2	1
4 Followed conventions for correct spelling, punctuation, sentence structure, and paragraphing	5	4	3	2	1

Total score: /20

Overall Level: Very High / High / Medium / Medium-Low / Low (Circle)

Comments:

_____

_____

_____

_____

_____

_____

_____

Writing in Context

Proofreading refers to checking a written or typed draft carefully for mistakes. After you handwrite or type your thoughts, you should check your writing for errors in four main areas:

- punctuation
- grammar
- spelling
- paragraph structure

When you check your writing for mistakes, you are learning the habit of being thorough. Thorough proofreading helps you achieve your best and impresses your readers, such as your teacher, friends and classmates, or parents. If you master all the lessons in this workbook, you will be able to avoid and correct common mistakes in writing.

Try It Out

Check the paragraph below for nine errors in punctuation, grammar, and spelling. Circle the mistakes in pencil. Then, rewrite the paragraph, including all nine corrections.

My dad bought her home as a suprise gift on my eigth birthday I was so excited. I love my dear dog Scruffy. She is so cute when she tilts her head to the left for a dog biscut. Shes a bit fat now as a result. She have been in our family for five years.

My dad brought her home as a surprise gift on my eighth birthday. I was so

excited. I love my dear dog Scruffy. She is so cute when she tilts her head to

the left for a dog biscuit. She's a bit fat now as a result. She has been in our

family for five years.

Taking It Further

Now that you have identified mistakes in spelling, punctuation, and grammar, it is time to complete the fifth area of mistakes: paragraph structure.

Which sentence in the paragraph on the previoius page states the topic? Underline it. That sentence should go first. Which supporting sentence is out of sequence? Circle it and then write the reordered paragraph below.

I love my dear dog Scruffy. My dad brought her home as a surprise gift on my

eighth birthday. I was so excited. She has been in our family for five years. She

is so cute when she tilts her head to the left for a dog biscuit. She's a bit fat

now as a result.

In the Real World

In pairs, exchange one or two paragraphs of your writing that have not been corrected by a teacher. Use a pencil to mark all mistakes in spelling, punctuation, grammar, and paragraph structure, and list them below. Then, rewrite your corrected version on a separate piece of paper and discuss the mistakes in pairs. Be thorough!

List of Improvements

Answers will vary.

_____

_____

_____

_____

_____

_____

_____

_____

Acknowledgements

The authors and publishers gratefully acknowledge Allen & Unwin for permission to use a passage from An Na's *A Step from Heaven* (Sydney 2000) on page 34.

Go Grammar!